Waheguru Pal Singh Sidhu

Enhancing Indo-US Strategic Cooperation

Adelphi Paper 313

Oxford University Press, Great Clarendon Street, Oxford OX2 6DP
Oxford New York
Athens Auckland Bangkok Bombay Calcutta Cape Town
Dar es Salaam Delhi Florence Hong Kong Istanbul Karachi
Kuala Lumpur Madras Madrid Melbourne Mexico City
Nairobi Paris Singapore Taipei Tokyo Toronto
and associated companies in
Berlin Ibadan

Oxford is a trade mark of Oxford University Press

Published in the United States
by Oxford University Press Inc., New York

© The International Institute for Strategic Studies 1997

First published September 1997 by **Oxford University Press** for
The International Institute for Strategic Studies
23 Tavistock Street, London WC2E 7NQ
http://www.isn.ethz.ch/iiss

Director John Chipman
Deputy Director Rose Gottemoeller
Editor Gerald Segal
Assistant Editor Matthew Foley
Design and Production Mark Taylor

British Library Cataloguing in Publication Data
Data available

Library of Congress Cataloguing in Publication Data

ISBN 0-19-829409-3
ISSN 0567-932x

contents

maps & figures

ACDA	Arms Control and Disarmament Agency (US)
AEC	Atomic Energy Commission
AERC	Atomic Energy Research Committee (India)
ASEAN	Association of South-East Asian Nations
ATM	Anti-tank missile
BARC	Bhabha Atomic Research Centre (India)
BIRD	Bi-national Industry Research and Development programme
BJP	*Bharatiya Janata* Party (India)
BMD	Ballistic-missile defence
CAVCTS	Combined Acceleration Vibration Climatic Test System
CCL	Commodities Control List (US)
CIA	Central Intelligence Agency (US)
CTBT	Comprehensive Test Ban Treaty
CUS	Cryogenic Upper Stage
CWC	Chemical Weapons Convention
DAE	Department of Atomic Energy (India)
DOD	Department of Defense (US)
DOE	Department of Energy (US)
DOS	Department of Space (India)
DPG	Defence Policy Group
DRDL	Defence Research and Development Laboratory (India)
DRDO	Defence Research and Development Organisation (India)
DST	Department of Science and Technology (India)
EAR	Export Administration Regulations
FMS	Foreign Military Sales

G-7 .... Group of Seven advanced industrialised nations
GTRE .... Gas Turbine Research Establishment (India)
IAEA .... International Atomic Energy Agency
ICBM .... Inter-continental ballistic missile
ICIA .... Import Certificate Issuing Authority
IGMDP .... Integrated Guided Missile Development
                         Programme
INSAT .... Indian National Satellite
IRBM .... Intermediate-range ballistic missile
IRS .... Indian Remote Sensing satellite
ISRO .... Indian Space Research Organisation
JSC .... Joint Steering Committee
JTG .... Joint Technical Group
LCA .... Light combat aircraft
LOA .... Letter of Offer and Acceptance
MBT .... Main battle tank
MEA .... Ministry of External Affairs (India)
MOU .... Memorandum of Understanding
MTCR .... Missile Technology Control Regime
NASA .... National Aeronautics and Space Administration
                         (US)
NNPA .... Nuclear Non-Proliferation Act (US)
NOAA .... National Oceanic and Atmospheric
                         Administration (US)
NPT .... Nuclear Non-Proliferation Treaty
NSA .... National Security Agency (US)
NSDD .... National Security Decision Directive (US)
NSG .... Nuclear Suppliers' Group
NTR .... National Test Range (India)
OPCW .... Organisation for Prevention of Chemical
                         Weapons
PACER .... Program for the Acceleration of Commercial
                         Energy Research
PACT .... Program for Acceleration of Commercial
                         Technology
PGM .... Precision-guided munition
PHWR .... Pressurised heavy water reactor
PNE .... Peaceful nuclear explosion
PPA .... Prevention of Proliferation Act (US)
PPP .... Purchasing-power parity
QR .... Quantitative Restriction
SAM .... Surface-to-air missile
SITE .... Satellite Instructional Television Experiment
SLV .... Satellite launch vehicle
SNEP .... Subterranean nuclear explosion project

SSM .... Surface-to-surface missile
STI .... Science and Technology Initiative
TIFR .... Tata Institute for Fundamental Research (India)
UAV .... Unmanned aerial vehicle
UNSC .... UN Security Council
USAID .... US Agency for International Development
USAPAC .... US Army Pacific Command
WMD .... Weapons of Mass Destruction
WTO .... World Trade Organisation

Defiance versus Accommodation

India enters its 51st year of independence displaying two distinct and apparently contradictory tendencies. The first, driven by regional security concerns – particularly potential military collaboration between China and Pakistan – is introverted, isolationist and belligerent. This translates into New Delhi's nuclear-weapon and missile programme and growing defiance of international nuclear non-proliferation regimes. The second, prompted by economic considerations – particularly the desire to integrate with the world economy – is extrovert, globalising and accommodative. This is reflected in India's economic liberalisation programme, which began in 1991 and has continued despite minority governments and several changes in leadership, and in its enthusiasm for regional economic groupings.

India's relations with the US exemplify these dual impulses. The US is India's largest foreign investor and trading partner.[1] However, this burgeoning economic relationship could falter if India – driven by security concerns – were to weaponise its nuclear capability. The US could impose sanctions under the 1994 Prevention of Proliferation Act (PPA), which could stall India's reform programme. These twin trends therefore represent both an opportunity and a threat. India, shedding years of isolation and keen to integrate with the expanding global economy, may adopt more cooperative policies. But, if this economic liberalisation and global integration is bought at the cost of its national security, India may slip back into isolationism.[2] There is, however, a third possibility: that the two tracks may run in parallel. Indo-US economic and political–military relations actually improved throughout bitter Comprehensive Test Ban Treaty (CTBT) negotiations in 1995–96 and a US embargo on the Indian Space Research Organisation (ISRO) in 1992–94.

The challenge before Washington and New Delhi is to find an innovative approach to their relations that boosts Indian economic interdependence and prosperity without sacrificing the country's national-security concerns. A fresh approach by the US to nuclear non-proliferation is central to this project. Traditionally, non-proliferation efforts have been pursued through sanctions and restrictions based on the Nuclear Non-Proliferation Treaty (NPT) and instruments such as the Nuclear Suppliers' Group (NSG) and the Missile Technology Control Regime (MTCR). However, even the US has recognised that, to deal with this issue in South Asia, domestic political concerns and regional security-threat perceptions must be taken into account.[3]

There are several reasons why this study focuses exclusively on India and the US. The World Bank has labelled India, which accounts for 80% of South Asia's gross domestic product (GDP), one of the 'fast integrators' of the global economy.[4] The US has identified India as one of the world's ten Big Emerging Markets.[5] Although trade and investment between India and Europe and India and the Association of South-East Asian Nations (ASEAN) may eventually exceed that between India and the US, Indo-US trade is currently greater than both.[6] The US is India's preferred source of technology.[7] India's size and location make it a key player in South Asia's strategic future, just as the US is the most significant actor in the global arena. The US and India are the world's largest democracies.

India and the US enjoy a long history of cooperation and share close economic, technological and political ties. But the two countries are at loggerheads over nuclear non-proliferation. The US leads the non-proliferation brigade; India heads the charge against what it considers to be discriminatory regimes. Given these opposing positions, is increased strategic cooperation possible? In this paper, the term 'strategic' is used to denote grand strategy, which includes military as well as non-military components.[8] What shape would cooperation take?[9] Must the two sides establish long-term goals – or can the relationship develop in their absence? Would it be commercial, government-to-government, or a blend of the two? What incentives could India offer to facilitate this new level of cooperation – and what would be its benefits?[10]

India's strategic and nuclear-weapon behaviour is driven by legitimate security concerns, technological and scientific lobbies and domestic politics. A new strategic relationship cannot be established without addressing these issues. Given the history of Indo-US cooperation and the current state of ties between the two, a 'stick-only' non-proliferation policy is neither desirable nor likely. However, as long as a gulf persists between the long-term interests of Washington and New Delhi, the prospects for a close strategic relationship (a 'carrot-only' partnership) are slim. While strategic defiance does not seem in prospect, a general trend towards increased strategic accommodation, albeit with some areas of friction, is likely to emerge.

chapter 1

A Rationale for India's Nuclear Option

Why do countries 'go nuclear'? India is not alone in citing several factors to justify its nuclear-weapon capability, among them security considerations, technical and scientific prowess and national prestige.[1] Scholars have also pointed out the importance of domestic political and bureaucratic considerations.[2] How valid are these claims and what is their impact on India's nuclear behaviour?

National-Security Concerns

India's national-security concerns are based on its location, history and complex domestic economic, social and political situation. The country's antagonistic relations with its undemocratic (or democratically fragile) neighbours and with the major global powers of the post-war era have also played an important part in shaping Indian threat perceptions. India's security concerns have varied at different points in its independent history. Threats have ranged from the purely military and predominantly territorial to questions of ideology, economics and prestige. Changes in the country's regional influence have also played a role. As the threats have varied, so have India's responses to them.

Border issues – primarily the result of the colonial legacy – are India's main national-security concern; nearly 7,000 kilometres of its 16,500km land border is disputed. A border dispute caused the 1962 Sino-Indian war, India's first military defeat. The war left the border issue unresolved and revealed the limitations of India's conventional military capabilities. The reluctance of external powers, particularly the US, to intervene militarily – despite pleas to do so – was to determine India's future desire for self-reliance in security needs.[3]

Persistent fears for state integrity have been compounded when the enemy within is seen to be acting in tandem with the enemy without.[4] This was the case in Punjab in the 1980s, and appears to be so in 1990s Kashmir, perhaps explaining why the 'end of the Cold War has not resulted in a peace dividend' for India.[5]

The nuclear-weapon capabilities of India's traditional regional adversaries – Pakistan and China – have also played a significant role in shaping India's strategic posture, including its nuclear-weapon aspirations and its relations with other powers, particularly the US. New Delhi's suspicions that China has aided Pakistan's nuclear and missile programme have sharpened the issue and created a triangular security relationship among the three. While China's growing nuclear arsenal spurs on India's weapon pro-gramme, Pakistan cites Indian capabilities as justification for its nuclear-weapon quest. The complications of this three-way relation-ship are crucial to understanding the rationale behind India's strategic policy.

The first Chinese nuclear test took place just two years after it defeated India in 1962.[6] As a result, New Delhi embarked on its first serious attempt to acquire a nuclear-weapon capability through the subterranean nuclear explosion project (SNEP), approved in December 1965.[7] Since the late 1980s, China's nuclear weapons have once again become an important rationale for India's nuclear and missile capability as reports emerged of tactical nuclear-missile deploy-ments in Tibet.[8] According to one estimate, three missile divisions had been deployed in the Lanzhou-Chengdu region.[9] Indian military officers claimed that 'China has already deployed intermediate-range ballistic missiles [IRBMs] in the Tibetan Plateau'.[10] Recent US intelligence reports support this assertion.[11]

the Chinese 'threat'

Apart from the direct threat posed by the Chinese nuclear arsenal, India also cites the indirect danger presented by Beijing's export of nuclear-weapon technology and delivery systems to countries in the region. Chinese assistance in Pakistan's nuclear and

Map I *India–China–Pakistan Missile Ranges*

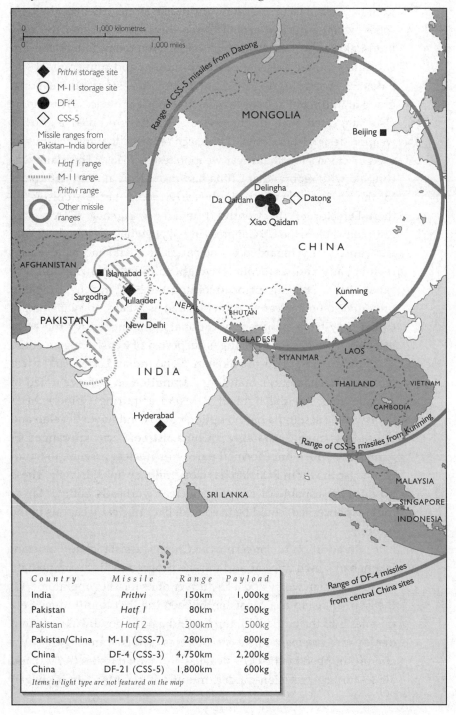

Country	Missile	Range	Payload
India	*Prithvi*	150km	1,000kg
Pakistan	*Hatf 1*	80km	500kg
Pakistan	*Hatf 2*	300km	500kg
Pakistan/China	M-11 (CSS-7)	280km	800kg
China	DF-4 (CSS-3)	4,750km	2,200kg
China	DF-21 (CSS-5)	1,800km	600kg
Items in light type are not featured on the map			

Legend:
- ◆ *Prithvi* storage site
- ○ M-11 storage site
- ● DF-4
- ◇ CSS-5

Missile ranges from Pakistan–India border
- *Hatf 1* range
- M-11 range
- *Prithvi* range
- Other missile ranges

missile programme is of specific concern: a possible Sino-Pakistani front has been a recurring worry for Indian strategists since the mid-1960s, when a nuclear-armed China threatened to enter the 1965 Indo-Pakistan war on Islamabad's side. Even today, India's concern is China's military assistance – both nuclear and conventional – to Pakistan. According to one report, China has supplied weapons-grade uranium to Pakistan to make two nuclear devices. This report also suggested that, in the 1980s, 'Pakistan received a proven weapon design from China. It has been reported that the design was used in China's fourth nuclear weapon test in 1966'.[12] This claim was coupled with reports that China had provided Pakistan with parts for the M-11 mobile missile in the early 1990s.[13] James Woolsey, the then Director of the Central Intelligence Agency (CIA), gave testimony before the US Congress in 1993 in which he noted: 'Beijing has consistently regarded a nuclear-armed Pakistan as a crucial regional ally and vital counterweight to India's growing military capabilities ... Beijing, prior to joining the NPT in 1992, probably provided some nuclear weapons-related assistance to Islamabad.'[14] China may have supplied 'additional components' for the M-11 missiles even *after* 1992; Beijing is suspected of transferring an entire M-11 production plant to Pakistan.[15] The Indian *Lok Sabha* (Lower House of Parliament)'s Standing Committee on Defence noted in August 1995: 'In the light of Pakistan acquiring Chinese M-11 ballistic missiles, India has no option but to continue to develop and upgrade its missile capability.'[16] China also sold 2,700km-range DF-3 missiles, which once formed part of its nuclear arsenal, to Saudi Arabia (with whom Pakistan has close military links) in 1987. These missiles are capable of carrying nuclear warheads and, as far as India is concerned, could be used to deliver nuclear weapons in the future.[17]

In addition to concern over China's assistance to Pakistan, Islamabad's own nuclear and missile programme is an immediate cause for Indian worry and a key driver of its missile programme. Of the two, Pakistan has consistently been the first to introduce new missiles into the battlefield, forcing India to respond. Pakistan first deployed *Sidewinder* air-to-air missiles, which came with F-104 aircraft supplied by the US, as well as anti-tank missiles (ATMs) and air-to-surface precision-guided munitions (PGMs).[18] India began seriously to examine surface-to-surface missiles (SSMs) only after their use in the Iran–Iraq war and Pakistan's reported interest in similar missiles with chemical warheads. General Mirza Aslam Beg, the former Chief of the Pakistan Army Staff, argued that India's missile programme is a response to Pakistan's:

> It [the Prithvi *short-range ballistic missile*] *is in response to what we have on our side. We have* Hatf, *which we deployed some three years ago. And at that time they* [India] *had nothing on the ground. So they have deployed in response to that. We don't blame them ... I think it is just to maintain balance.*[19]

Indian reports in June 1997 cited the need to maintain 'balance' to justify the forward storage of the *Prithvi* at Jullander, close to the Pakistani border, in response to the storage of M-11s at Sargodha.[20] However, the lengthy development period for both sides' missiles and their simultaneous appearance in the late 1980s suggest that India and Pakistan launched their programmes at around the same time. The original Indian missile programme began in the 1970s. Statements by then Pakistani Prime Minister Benazir Bhutto at the time of the successful launch of the 80km-range *Hatf* 1 and the 300km *Hatf* 2 in early 1989 indicated that these missiles were the fruit of a project initiated in 1974 by her father, Prime Minister Zulfiqar Ali Bhutto, on a 'priority basis'.[21]

India also points to the presence of nuclear weapons in the Indian Ocean and the former Soviet Union, particularly 'loose nukes' in Central Asia, to justify its nuclear project. New Delhi has become especially sensitive to the presence of nuclear weapons in the Indian Ocean following the 1971 *USS Enterprise* episode. In the midst of the 1971 Indo-Pakistan war which led to the creation of Bangladesh, the US National Security Council despatched the Pacific 7th Fleet, designated as Task Force 74, to the Bay of Bengal, which it reached on 13 December, five days before the war ended. The force, led by the *Enterprise*, remained 1,760km from Dhaka until January 1972, when it set sail for the Pacific. The objective of the US in deploying Task Force 74 occupies analysts to this day. Perhaps one of the most credible explanations is that offered by Henry Kissinger,

Map 2 *Indian Nuclear Establishments*

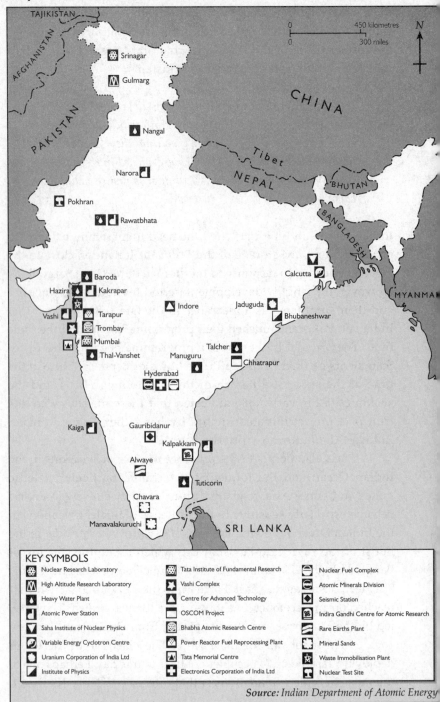

KEY SYMBOLS

Nuclear Research Laboratory	Tata Institute of Fundamental Research	Nuclear Fuel Complex
High Altitude Research Laboratory	Vashi Complex	Atomic Minerals Division
Heavy Water Plant	Centre for Advanced Technology	Seismic Station
Atomic Power Station	OSCOM Project	Indira Gandhi Centre for Atomic Research
Saha Institute of Nuclear Physics	Bhabha Atomic Research Centre	Rare Earths Plant
Variable Energy Cyclotron Centre	Power Reactor Fuel Reprocessing Plant	Mineral Sands
Uranium Corporation of India Ltd	Tata Memorial Centre	Waste Immobilisation Plant
Institute of Physics	Electronics Corporation of India Ltd	Nuclear Test Site

Source: Indian Department of Atomic Energy

Secretary of State at the time, who claimed that the move was designed not only to 'assist' Pakistan, but also to 'back up the Chinese'. For the Indians, however, the 1971 intrusion was a form of gunboat diplomacy. As one scholar noted: 'The sailing of the *USS Enterprise* was the ultimate in symbolic insult ... Above all, it is remembered as a nuclear as well as a military threat.'[22] Subsequent Indian naval doctrine spoke of 'raising the cost of intervention' and, although it did not elaborate on what that would entail, strategists have argued in favour of a nuclear-powered submarine armed with nuclear or conventional missiles.[23]

Fears of an extra-regional nuclear power threatening India rose again in the early 1990s, when General Dynamics Corporation, makers of the *Tomahawk* land-attack cruise missile, gave a presentation to US decision-makers which portrayed a scenario in which the US might retaliate against an Indian attack on Pakistan by firing hundreds of *Tomahawks* at military and industrial sites in India. Reports of the presentation in the Indian press provoked a diplomatic clash between the US and India, which some Indians saw as part of a US desire to threaten India.[24] While these concerns pose varied degrees of nuclear threat, New Delhi currently has no weaponised deterrent capability.

The Technical and Scientific Impetus

India's high-technology institutions, like those elsewhere, have developed their own momentum. This is particularly the case in those institutions related to the nuclear, missile and space fields. This momentum is the result partly of a quest for technological development for its own sake, partly to justify the investment in infrastructure and personnel made in these establishments and partly to meet security needs.

Independent India gave the highest priority to atomic science. Jawaharlal Nehru, India's first Prime Minister, and Dr Homi Jehangir Bhabha, who led the atomic bureaucracy, set up the Atomic Energy Research Committee (AERC) to promote research in nuclear physics at Indian universities as early as 1946. Nehru chaired the first meeting of the AERC just 12 days after independence. The Atomic Energy Commission (AEC) was established in August 1948 under the provisions of the Atomic Energy Act, passed the previous

April – less than a year after independence.[25] By the time the Department of Atomic Energy (DAE) was established in 1954, Bhabha had drawn up an elaborate three-stage nuclear-power programme to make use of India's limited uranium and vast thorium resources. In 1956, Apsara, India's first reactor (and the first in Asia outside the Soviet Union) went critical. By mid-1960, India was generating nuclear power and was able to build its own reactors. In 1997, India's ten nuclear-power reactors produce 1,695MW of the country's total installed capacity of 83,000MW.[26]

The 'weapon-option' policy determined the extent of India's nuclear-weapon capabilities. In its simplest form, this policy meant that India would develop the basic technical wherewithal to give it the option to build a weapon in a reasonable time if it felt the need to do so.[27] The policy appears to have been put in place by Prime Minister Nehru, even though the capability to exercise it seems to have been attained under his successors. India was able to manufacture fissile material and reprocess plutonium by the mid-1960s, and the country's only nuclear test took place in 1974. The 100MW Dhruva reactor, capable of supplying 20–25 kilograms of weapons-grade plutonium a year, was commissioned in 1985; a plant capable of reprocessing 100 tonnes of plutonium a year followed. According to the 'most conservative' figure, India has the capability to manufacture 60 nuclear bombs.[28]

Today, the AEC employs more than 15,000 scientists and engineers in four government research centres alone.[29] Although most research the peaceful applications of nuclear energy, particularly in the power, medical and agricultural sectors, a significant number of personnel work on technology directly related to nuclear weapons. This group is likely to push for India to move further down the weaponisation path as this would be directly related to their own professional success.[30] It is no coincidence that the three key scientists involved with India's 1974 nuclear test – Dr Raja Ramanna, Dr P. K. Iyengar and Dr R. Chidambaram – all became chairmen of the AEC. Younger AEC scientists were the most vocal in calling for a nuclear test in late 1995 and early 1996.[31] Although some in India claimed that it was justified on both technical and military grounds, no test took place.

Similarly, the impetus for the missile programme comes from the scientists and technologists involved with the Integrated Guided

Missile Development Programme (IGMDP), launched in 1983, as well as the personnel of the Defence Research and Development Organisation (DRDO), who also stand to benefit from continued patronage. The DRDO was formally established on 1 January 1958, although defence research and development had been under way since 1948. Today, the DRDO comprises 50 laboratories and establishments and about 15 air-worthiness certification centres and employs about 30,000 people. Of these, only 6,800 are scientific and technical personnel. DRDO establishments are spread throughout the country, although half are sited in three cities, New Delhi, Bangalore and Hyderabad.[32] Of the DRDO's projects, pride of place belongs to the IGMDP, particularly its nuclear-capable *Prithvi* and *Agni* missiles.

Although now regarded as symbols of the nation's technical prowess and military strength, the origins of the *Prithvi* and *Agni* were humble. The military missile programme was deliberately separated from the civilian space programme from its inception. The Defence Research and Development Laboratory (DRDL) in Hyderabad, the primary laboratory involved with missile research, predates the civil space programme by at least four years.[33] According to a US intelligence assessment, the two programmes 'compete for resources'.[34] A 1988 US Embassy assessment notes:

> We believe that most ISRO scientists agree with the official policy of keeping separate India's military and civilian rocket programs. They argue that ISRO is not developing military missile technologies in its civilian space program even though certain technologies can be shared by both ... They are supported by defence scientists who maintain that using the ISRO rockets would involve major modifications, [and] that they would rather design and are designing military missiles from scratch.[35]

This is not to say that there is no cooperation or transfer of technology, and occasionally personnel, between the two programmes.[36] For example, Dr A. P. J. Abdul Kalam, who began his career in the DRDO, was seconded to the ISRO in the late 1970s to head the civilian satellite launch vehicle (SLV)-3 project. He later returned to the DRDO to lead the missile-development programme.

Map 3 *Organisations Participating in the IGMDP*

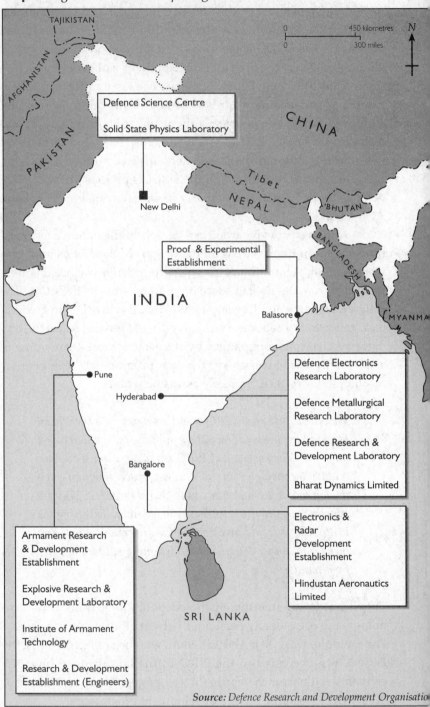

TAJIKISTAN

AFGHANISTAN

PAKISTAN

CHINA

Tibet

NEPAL

BHUTAN

BANGLADESH

MYANMA

INDIA

SRI LANKA

0   450 kilometres   N

0   300 miles

Defence Science Centre

Solid State Physics Laboratory

New Delhi

Proof & Experimental
Establishment

Balasore

Pune

Hyderabad

Bangalore

Defence Electronics
Research Laboratory

Defence Metallurgical
Research Laboratory

Defence Research &
Development Laboratory

Bharat Dynamics Limited

Electronics &
Radar
Development
Establishment

Hindustan Aeronautics
Limited

Armament Research
& Development
Establishment

Explosive Research &
Development Laboratory

Institute of Armament
Technology

Research & Development
Establishment (Engineers)

Source: Defence Research and Development Organisatio

The IGMDP set out to design and build five missiles. While three – the *Trishul* quick-reaction surface-to-air (SAM) missile, the *Akash* SAM and the *Nag* ATM – are purely conventional and tactical, the *Prithvi* and *Agni* are nuclear-capable and strategic in their reach.[37] The *Agni* is designated a 'technology demonstrator' and, although it has IRBM characteristics, was not built with a service requirement. It was clearly designed to carry a nuclear warhead to ranges of 1,500–2,500km (although in the three tests conducted to date, its range has been much shorter). The *Prithvi* SSM is described as a 'battlefield support missile' with a range of 40–250km. This puts it in the tactical and strategic bracket, especially in the Indo-Pakistani context.[38] In its present configuration the *Privthi* is purely conventional and can carry five different kinds of warheads, but its throw-weight of one ton makes it nuclear-capable.

Although each missile could have been allotted an individual programme, the government in 1983 approved a combined budget of Rs7 billion ($300 million) for all five and appointed Kalam programme head. Kalam offers one of the most lucid explanations as to why these missiles, particularly the tactical and strategic ones, were bracketed together:

> The logic was that if you take the IGMDP there is a relationship, technology-wise, there are some common technologies and instead of depending upon only your own strength, you assemble, you integrate the strength of the whole country.[39]

This reveals possibly inadequate political support for five individual missile programmes, which could therefore only be sold as a group. This strategy appears to have worked: those tactical-missile programmes which have slipped behind schedule have piggy-backed on the success of the *Prithvi*. Had these missiles been under development in individual programmes, funding may have been curtailed.

To exploit national strength and technological capabilities, Kalam, supported by the technocratic head of the DRDO, Dr V. S. Arunachalam, embarked on a 'consortium approach' which aimed to create a complex system comprising 'about 64 participating

institutions and five types of partners in the missile programme'.[40]
The five partners were:

- the users (the three armed services);
- 19 defence laboratories;
- other scientific institutions;
- academic institutions; and
- about 30 private and public industries.

This partnership approach was a marked departure from past
DRDO programmes, in which the technologies were developed as
much as possible in-house. The new participative system, which had
more in common with the ISRO's pattern of operations, made the
base of alliances much broader. This was the key to the success of the
IGMDP. While the 'consortium approach' may have been primarily
dictated by technological imperatives, there is little doubt that it
resulted in the creation of a strong alliance of vested interests – those
concerned about 'brain-drain' (the loss of skilled technicians and
scientists to other countries), missile engineers and nuclear-option
adherents – which ensured the success of the missile programme.

The impending MTCR also played a role in the emergence of
the 'consortium approach'. Although still several years away when
the IGMDP was launched in 1983, there were indications that such a
regime would come into force once India's nuclear-capable-missile
programme was unveiled.[41] India did not intend to eliminate
imports, but to ensure that certain 'critical components' were not
denied, especially after the MTCR came into force. As Kalam noted:

> *Once* Agni *was launched [we realised] there will be many
> countries which will stop some critical components. We
> anticipated the areas where they were going to throttle us and
> prepared to acquire the technology. We identified five critical
> components and we worked for two and a half years. In 1986
> the MTCR was formed. They cannot do anything to us. We
> are self-sufficient.*[42]

The five technologies Kalam identified were: phase shifters for
radar; impact diodes that act as high-frequency power-sources;

carbon composites to withstand the heat of re-entry; key sensors for guidance systems; and computerised fluid dynamic models.[43]

The 'consortium approach' reduced the design–testing–production cycle to a mere eight years and, by pooling expertise, development costs remained affordable. The creation of the consortium also increased the stakes of the participating agencies in the success of the missile programme. The IGMDP was hailed a success immediately after the maiden test of the *Prithvi* on 28 February 1988. So certain were the scientists of the missile's performance that, soon after the first launch, they abandoned their three planned experimental flights to test propulsion, guidance and control and embarked directly on the development-trial phase. In the *Prithvi* programme of 16 tests to date, only one has failed.

The success of the *Prithvi* and *Agni* programmes should not be seen in isolation but in the broader context of other ambitious DRDO projects which have fallen far behind schedule.[44] The *Prithvi*'s success is critical to continued funding for, and patronage of, the DRDO. It is, therefore, in the interest of the DRDO (and the other agencies that participated in the IGMDP) to promote the *Prithvi* and to ensure that it enters production and is deployed. This would also help to counter the frequent charge that the DRDO has been unable to put most of its systems into production.

Symbols of Prestige

Indians regard their country's nuclear and missile programmes as symbols of technical prowess and scientific competence, particularly in contrast to the generally low level of technology and development in other sectors. For a developing country like India, expertise in nuclear and missile technology proves its grasp of high technology, not only reflecting the nation's technical potential, but also placing it alongside the world's leading developed nations. Indian analysts point out that the permanent members of the UN Security Council (UNSC) are also the five officially recognised nuclear-weapon states. In doing so, these analysts are making a strong case that nuclear and missile technology is necessary if a country is to be regarded as equal to the most powerful in the world. As DRDO head Kalam is fond of saying: 'Strength respects strength. When a country is technologically strong other countries will respect it'.[45]

These programmes – and the technical expertise they call for – are also considered essential to bolster India's criticism of the numerous sanction regimes, which it considers discriminatory. India's expertise in the nuclear and missile fields gives it the ability to challenge these regimes. One of the official mandates laid down for the DRDO is 'to develop critical components, technologies ... and to reduce the vulnerability of major programmes ... from various embargoes/denial regimes, instituted by advanced countries'.[46] Consequently, India has tried to ensure that the impact of such sanctions is low. Although some programmes suffered in the short term because of sanctions, in the long term these 'denial regimes' boosted India's desire for self-reliance. Indian nuclear scientists are proud of having overcome what they consider unfair impediments to their primarily peaceful programme.[47] International Atomic Energy Agency (IAEA) Director Hans Blix acknowledged as much when he noted that 'when you think of self-reliance, there is no better example than India'.[48]

Domestic Pressures

The nuclear issue does not feature among Indians' top concerns. According to a survey in late 1994, only 6% of respondents considered the nuclear issue to be of the greatest priority. It ranked seventh after communalism (52%); poverty (47%); economic stability (36%); terrorism (30%); Kashmir (15%); and the General Agreement on Tariffs and Trade (GATT – 8%).[49] And yet, every time a survey by the Indian Institute for Public Opinion focuses exclusively on the nuclear issue, over 50% consistently support developing a bomb. In 1968, 73% supported building a bomb; in 1970, it had dropped to 68%. A survey in 1974, soon after the country's nuclear test, revealed that 75% of respondents favoured the bomb option. In 1987, 53% were in favour if Pakistan developed a nuclear device, while a survey in 1992 showed that 56% felt that India should develop nuclear weapons.[50] The 1994 survey, which was confined to India's élite, revealed that 57% of those polled favoured New Delhi's policy of 'neither confirming nor denying a *de facto* nuclear capability while espousing global nuclear disarmament'.[51]

consistent support for a nuclear option

The armed forces also support India's nuclear option. The Army has demanded nuclear weapons since the mid-1960s, but has so far not only been denied its wish, but has also been excluded from nuclear decision-making.[52] However, as the Army becomes more vocal in its demands for nuclear weapons and nuclear-capable missiles, this situation may change. During the winter of 1995–96, reports suggested that the planned nuclear test was for military – as well as technical – purposes.[53] Former Army officers have welcomed the more recent decision to 'defreeze' the *Agni* programme.[54] As one Indian analyst noted, were the Army to become more 'involved in shaping the strategy, the nuclear stance would harden'.[55]

India's nuclear-weapon policy therefore appears to be driven as much by domestic political considerations as by external threat-perceptions and the scientific and technocratic impetus. Despite vociferous debate about the nuclear issue from 1964, the final decision to test in 1974 appeared to have been taken by Prime Minister Indira Gandhi for domestic political reasons. Her popularity had begun to wane following her general-election victory after the 1971 war with Pakistan, and she faced challenges to her authority.[56] She therefore used the nuclear test, which was presented as an achievement of Indian science and technology and identified with the ruling Congress party, to bolster her position.[57] Similarly, Prime Minister Rajiv Gandhi's administration ran a series of advertisements on *Doordarshan*, the government-controlled electronic media, in the run-up to the 1989 elections extolling India as a great nation, a responsible regional peacekeeper – and capable of manufacturing missiles like the *Agni* and building nuclear-power stations.[58]

If governments with majorities, like those of the Gandhis, depended on achievements in the nuclear and missile fields to buttress their regimes, it is even more important that minority governments are not seen to be compromising on the nuclear issue. The 1996 election saw the right-wing Hindu nationalist *Bharatiya Janata* Party (BJP) use India's nuclear capability as an election issue when it pledged to 're-evaluate the country's nuclear policy and exercise the option to induct nuclear weapons'.[59] Prime Minister P. V. Narasimha Rao's minority administration responded by assuring the electorate that there would be no compromise on the nuclear issue.

The domestic impetus for India's nuclear posture was particularly evident during the CTBT negotiations. India, which had originally co-sponsored the resolution in 1993, blocked the Treaty when it was ready to be put to the vote in 1996. According to one scholar, the US directly pressured Rao through the Prime Minister's office, bypassing the Ministry of External Affairs (MEA), in a bid to convince India to sign – or at least not to block – the Treaty.[60] Rao apparently acceded to offset pressure from Washington, whose official policy called for India to 'cap, freeze and roll back' its nuclear programme. Rao may also have backed down in the belief that the CTBT would not succeed given the serious differences between some nuclear-weapon states, notably France and China. The belief that the Treaty would not work was revealed by a senior Indian diplomat in 1994.[61] India and the US reached an understanding whereby India would not block the CTBT, make a token amendment to it and cut funding for the *Prithvi* and *Agni* programmes, while the US would ease the pressure on Indo-Pakistani denuclearisation. It was thought that Rao would be able to deliver on the deal after *Lok Sabha* elections in 1996. However, the US failed to take into account the role and impact of public opinion and the parliamentary process in India, while Rao misjudged his own political vulnerability, particularly in countering pro-nuclear BJP rhetoric and the coalition of pro-bomb nuclear scientists and MEA and Ministry of Defence (MOD) bureaucrats and technocrats.

Domestic pressure on the nuclear and missile issue in 1994–96 thus forced Rao to harden his stance on the CTBT.[62] In late 1995, India began to link the Treaty with global disarmament within a 'fixed time-frame', but the dramatic shift in India's CTBT position came in December that year with the leak of US intelligence reports claiming that preparatory work had been undertaken at the Pokhran nuclear test-site. The revelation was

hardening stance on the CTBT

particularly ill timed: it now seems clear that, although preparatory work was indeed carried out, 'no final decision had actually been made at this point' on whether to test or not.[63] Nevertheless, the reports sparked off intense domestic public debate which, in an election year, put nuclear policy high on the national agenda.[64] An opinion poll conducted around this time revealed that 62% of respondents approved of a nuclear test to develop India's nuclear-weapon capability.[65] Rao had no choice but to reaffirm that he would not compromise India's nuclear option.

India thus returned to the CTBT talks in January 1996 with a rigid and uncompromising stance which, as a high-risk, all-or-nothing strategy, clearly weakened its negotiating position. Rao may still have felt that the Treaty would in any case fail under the weight of the disagreements between the parties. However, reliance on this worst-case outcome left India without a fall-back negotiating position (as, for example, the Chinese had prepared) should the Treaty become reality. All India could do was veto it. Confronted by the impending 28 June 1996 deadline for finalising the CTBT draft, the new coalition government in New Delhi under H. D. Deve Gowda chose to continue the approach of its predecessor. Then Foreign Minister Inder Kumar Gujral reiterated that India was committed to realising an effective CTBT that would be a genuine instrument for global nuclear disarmament. He justified pressing on with the previous government's policy on the grounds that it reflected the 'thrust of the election manifestos of major political parties' that had contested the 1996 elections.[66] On 20 June, Foreign Secretary Salman Haider declared that preserving national security led New Delhi formally to reject the CTBT in its present form. He pointed out that India was unwilling to give up its nuclear-weapon option unilaterally, especially as the CTBT did not improve the security environment in South Asia.[67] Significantly, however, the weapon option came under severe pressure in the run-up to the CTBT deadline. Several key players – the nuclear bureaucracy, the MOD, sections of the MEA and the media as well as the ardently pro-nuclear BJP – pressed for a test and subsequent overt weaponisation. Nevertheless, the weapon-option policy survived. This indicates not only its resilience, but also the pro-bomb alliance's inability to push for overt weaponisation.

One of the strengths of India's nuclear-weapon and missile capability is that it is popularly seen as a symbol of the country's power and high-technology status. However, if economic reforms succeed and India becomes a substantial economic and technological player, economic success may become the new currency of power, displacing nuclear-weapon technology – as is the case with Germany and Japan. Then, perhaps, India may not feel the need to proceed down the proliferation path, even if it has the wherewithal to do so. However, to ensure that there is no further movement towards overt weaponisation, India, like Germany and Japan, would have to be certain that its security was assured.

New Delhi's reluctance to accept external security guarantees means that, to ensure security via non-nuclear means, its conventional capabilities must be enhanced through technology cooperation. Alternatively, India's latent deterrent capability based on the nuclear-weapon option would have to be recognised. The US and Israel cooperate, particularly in ballistic-missile-defence (BMD) systems such as the *Arrow*; some analysts have proposed a similar arrangement for India.[68] Official Indian strategists have expressed reservations on the grounds that China, which sees BMD as a means to curtail its deterrent edge, may not welcome such cooperation.[69] These strategists argue that such a move could work only if it is an interim measure towards the goal of a 'zero missile regime'.[70]

Conditions for Cooperation

It is clear that a successful bid to deepen cooperation between India and the US would have to satisfy several conditions. First, it would have to ensure that India's security is not compromised. One way to achieve this would be to provide access to high-technology conventional weaponry, which would effectively deter even a nuclear threat. However, this is a difficult proposition given that the US may be unwilling to share the cutting-edge conventional technology that could deter nuclear attack. Alternatively, recognition of India's nascent nuclear-deterrence capability as an interim measure to ensure its security, with abolition of all nuclear weapons as the ultimate objective, would also pave the way for closer cooperation. Another way of ensuring India's security would be to reduce and eventually eliminate the nuclear threat it faces, particularly that posed by China and Pakistan. This could be attempted by engaging both countries at bilateral, regional and multilateral levels, and by creating a global, non-discriminatory regime committed to the elimination of nuclear weapons. It is significant that this is the model that India followed in its approach to the Chemical Weapons Convention (CWC), where regional concerns were dovetailed into a global non-discriminatory treaty. However, in the nuclear field, this cohesion between regional and global concerns would be difficult to achieve given that the existing NPT is clearly discriminatory.

The second precondition would be to satisfy domestic political lobbies, which currently see India's nuclear-weapon capability as vital for security and symbolic of sovereignty and status within the community of nations. Nuclear capability would need to be replaced by an equally potent symbol, such as a vibrant economy, a greater regional role and, perhaps, a permanent seat on the UNSC. While closer Indo-US cooperation would not necessarily guarantee India's economic prowess, its regional position or a UNSC seat, it would facilitate the process. US support may also provide a lead for others to follow.

One of the major bottlenecks in Indian economic growth is the lack of adequate infrastructure, particularly in energy and transport (according to one estimate, the shortfall in power supplies could result in the loss of 6% of GDP a year).[71] If Indo-US cooperation paved the way for joint energy projects (perhaps including nuclear energy), it would boost the economy. Interestingly, most of the 'fast-track' power projects currently under consideration involve US companies.[72] The 2,015MW power project at Dabhol (Maharashtra), put together by three US companies – Enron, Bechtel and GE Capital – is a good test case for future cooperation.[73] However, while the economy shows all the signs of becoming a key component in India's power equation, there is still a long way to go before it can replace other apparent trappings of power.

In terms of India's South Asian role, the Gujral doctrine is indicative of the country's rise as a benign regional power. The doctrine, which emphasises economic cooperation and focuses on friendly relations with India's neighbours on a basis of mutual respect, has five basic principles.

• With neighbours such as Bangladesh, Bhutan, the Maldives, Nepal and Sri Lanka, India 'does not ask for reciprocity, but gives all it can in good faith'.
• No South Asian country will allow its territory to be used for

purposes which are 'against the interests of another country in the region'.

- No South Asian country will interfere in the internal affairs of another.
- All South Asian countries must 'respect each other's territorial integrity and sovereignty'.
- All will settle disputes 'peacefully through bilateral negotiations'.[74]

In the international arena, New Delhi's hopes of UNSC membership, which suffered a setback in 1996 with a defeat at the hands of Japan, revived in 1997 as the US voiced its support for an enlarged UNSC and declared that it would back membership for three 'developing countries', in addition to Germany and Japan.[75] Although Washington has officially shied away from formally supporting any one state and wants developing countries to decide among themselves who to propose, some US Congressmen have advocated India's case.[76]

The third requirement would be to channel the talent of India's nuclear and missile scientists into other equally advanced areas which would provide a vehicle for their professional skills. Suitable avenues could include joint research into non-lethal aspects of nuclear science and energy. Senior Indian nuclear scientists point to the collaboration between the Bhabha Atomic Research Centre (BARC) and the National Accelerator Laboratory at Brookhaven (New York) in a quark experiment in the

embracing non-lethal science

1980s. The experiment was funded by the US Department of Energy (DOE) and India's Tata Institute for Fundamental Research (TIFR).[77] India was hopeful that this cooperation could be increased, and was willing to invest $50m in a super-collider project with a laboratory in Texas. However, the project, which had been supported by the Bush administration, was cancelled by the Clinton government, which took office in 1992.

Even foreign investment in non-nuclear but high-technology industries in India has slowed work on strategic military projects. Lured by better salaries and working conditions, there has been a large exodus of talented scientists from crucial defence projects, such as the light combat aircraft (LCA), missile and radar systems and high-speed computers, to multinational companies. The rate at which scientists are leaving varies from 8–20% of the DRDO's total scientific manpower.[78]

There is, clearly, a case for India to retain its nuclear-weapon option because of political, military and technological considerations. This weapon-option policy could alter should the conditions that determined it change. Closer Indo-US strategic cooperation, with the implicit political, military, technological and economic affinity that it would entail, could facilitate this change. However, as the next chapter explains, past attempts at such cooperation have met with limited success.

chapter 2

The Indo-US Cooperative Experience

India and the US share a 50-year history of technological and
scientific cooperation in agriculture, space research, nuclear energy
and military technology. This cooperation has included food and
technical assistance for India's 'green revolution' in the 1950s and
1960s; fuel for its first nuclear-power plant at Tarapur (commissioned in 1963); and the loan of satellites followed by construction of
the Indian National Satellite (*INSAT*) series.[1] The motives for, and
the extent of, this cooperation have varied depending on several
factors, including India's domestic economic policies; its nuclear
posture; its relations with Pakistan, the former Soviet Union and the
US; and the priority accorded to non-proliferation, China and
Pakistan by Washington. Nevertheless, throughout the 50-year
relationship, Indo-US technology cooperation has never been
entirely absent.

A Brief History of Indo-US Cooperation
In the 1950s and 1960s, Indo-US cooperation focused on financial
and food aid, as well as agriculture and space and nuclear research.[2]
There are indications that shared anti-China sentiments partly
dictated this scientific and technological cooperation. The US also
offered military assistance to India during the 1962 Sino-Indian war,
although Washington's reluctance overtly to flex its muscles irked
Indian strategists. US unwillingness to institutionalise or expand
military cooperation on a long-term basis was seen as a sign of

unreliability and was to prompt India's subsequent quest for military self-reliance.[3] There is some indication that the US considered its assistance to India during this period, particularly in the agricultural and nuclear fields, as a means of influencing New Delhi's latent nuclear-weapon ambitions.[4] Michael Edwardes argued that India was deterred from conducting a nuclear test in the wake of China's test in 1964 because of the 'expressed disapproval' of the US, upon which India depended for grain under the PL-480 scheme.[5]

Even during the 1970s, Indo-US technology cooperation did not come to a standstill, despite a series of events and issues that complicated relations. These included: India's refusal to sign the NPT in 1968; the Nixon administration's discernible 'tilt' towards Pakistan during the 1971 Indo-Pakistani war; India's 'peaceful nuclear explosion' in 1974; and the passage of the US Nuclear Non-Proliferation Act (NNPA) in 1978. While cooperation was virtually non-existent in the nuclear and military-technology fields, it continued in space technology. The Indian Department of Space (DOS) conducted the Satellite Instructional Television Experiment (SITE) with the help of the US National Aeronautics and Space Administration (NASA), which loaned its ATS-6 satellite to beam programmes on health, education and agriculture to more than 5,000 villages. The lessons learnt from SITE played a significant role in the subsequent development of the *INSAT*-1 class of satellites. As these programmes grew in size, both governments agreed in 1974 to establish a joint commission to facilitate contacts in science, technology, education and culture.

cooperation despite conflict

This trend continued in the 1980s, despite the Soviet intervention in Afghanistan and the Carter and Reagan administrations' offer of military assistance to Pakistan, which adversely affected Indo-US political relations. The US became India's largest trading partner, particularly in high-technology categories – electronics, computers and telecommunications equipment. Trade volumes rose by 47% from $149m in 1985 to $220m in 1986.[6] In 1988, of total US exports to India of $2.5bn, high-technology items accounted for over a third (about $870m).[7] The dominant role of the US in supplying high technology was made possible by the Reagan–Gandhi Science and Technology Initiative (STI) in 1982 – which dealt with civil equipment – and a 1984 Memorandum of Understanding (MOU) on Sensitive Technologies, Commodities and Information, which dealt with military equipment.[8]

Nevertheless, the two countries' political relationship, particularly over nuclear and security issues, was acrimonious. Given that the traditional approach of both India and the US to the proliferation issue should have prevented such a *rapprochement*, how did this pragmatic relationship develop? And, more significantly, how did it work?

Indo-US Cooperation in the 1980s

Several factors led to the emergence of an Indo-US cooperative regime in the 1980s, despite the serious differences between the two countries. First, the personal rapport between Prime Minister Indira Gandhi and President Reagan, following their brief meeting at the North–South Economic Summit in Cancun (Mexico) in 1981, paved the way for increased Indo-US interaction, which continued during the tenure of Rajiv Gandhi.[9] There are several plausible reasons why the Gandhis chose to move close to the US during this period. Both had serious reservations about the Soviet intervention in Afghanistan, which they expressed privately to Moscow. India was particularly concerned that the Soviet action had made Pakistan a front-line state and created a US–Pakistan–China axis. India found the Cold War on its doorstep, and threatening to spill over into the subcontinent itself.

Second, the Soviet Union was now considered an unreliable supplier of advanced conventional weaponry. For example, when India's then Defence Minister, Ramaswamy Venkataraman, visited Moscow in 1983 and enquired about the new Soviet MiG-29 fighter, about which he had learnt from other sources, his hosts denied that it existed. But, barely six months later, they offered it for sale to India.[10] Venkataraman's experience was in marked contrast to past Indo-Soviet arms relations. From the mid-1960s, Moscow emerged as 'India's single most important supplier'.[11] In 1965–69, the Soviets supplied 80% of all Indian defence equipment; in the 1970s, their share fluctuated between 70% and 57%. Moscow was willing to offer New Delhi generous terms and agreements, granting long-term credits (from ten to 17 years) and charging low rates of interest (2–2.5%); repayments could be made by goods-exports rather than foreign exchange. Moscow also allowed licensed production and some technology transfer.[12]

Doubts about Soviet reliability as a supplier coincided with New Delhi's concern that India was too dependent on Soviet military hardware. The government therefore attempted to diversify and 'indigenise' sources of supply. Diversification led to Indian interest in the French *Mirage*-2000 aircraft, Germany's HDW Type 1500 submarine and the Swedish Bofors FH 155mm gun, all of which were eventually bought.[13] However, despite initial interest, India backed down from a similar deal to buy howitzers and TOW missile-launchers from the US. 'Indigenisation' saw the launch of three major DRDO weapon programmes: the LCA, which was to replace the MiG-21; the main battle tank (MBT) *Arjun*, which would succeed the *Vijayanta* and T-55 MBTs; and the IGMDP, which was to replace some Soviet SAMs. These programmes, particularly the LCA, appear to have been undertaken in the teeth of strong Soviet opposition. In a telling incident, then Defence Minister Marshal Dimitri Ustinov personally rebuked DRDO chief Arunachalam in 1982 for going ahead with the LCA project.[14]

Strategic and political issues apart, both Gandhis were personally cool towards the Soviets. Indira Gandhi felt let down by Moscow when she was out of power; her son possessed a closer affinity with the West and carried no pro-Soviet ideological baggage. India's desire to distance itself from the Soviet Union coincided with the US wish to make an 'opening' to India – a phrase used by mid- and high-level policy-makers in Washington in the mid-1980s.[15]

According to one US expert on South Asia, Washington had three major regional objectives: to contain Soviet power; to 'encourage Indian strategic autonomy (defined as a lessening of Indian dependence on the Soviet Union)'; and to prevent nuclear proliferation.[16] This convergence of interests, particularly with regard to the Soviet Union and technology, was crucial in developing Indo-US cooperation. It was also helped by the personal conviction of the key individuals involved – Arunachalam

the strategic logic for cooperation

and the US Under-Secretary of Defense for Policy, Fred Ikle – that cooperation would be mutually beneficial. Ikle, a conservative strategist, was convinced of the need to help India to develop its indigenous defence capabilities.[17] Arunachalam favoured the introduction of foreign technology and argued for 'flying the aircraft rather than flying the flag'.[18]

India's scientific and technical capabilities, particularly in the nuclear, space and defence industries, also matured in this period. By the early 1980s, India was building nuclear-power and research reactors; launching satellites and using them in applications ranging from mass-communications to remote sensing; and had embarked on several ambitious defence projects. These programmes were supported by India's political leadership, which provided adequate funding for the DRDO's indigenous programmes.[19] These programmes aimed 'not only to make India competent in the design and development of weapon systems, but also to empower the manufacturing sector to meet India's defence needs'.[20] India was thus competently handling existing technology – and was also seeking next-generation technology, which could only come from the US and Europe.

Indian *rapprochement* with the US was also seen as a counterpoise to the US–Pakistan strategic relationship which had emerged following the Soviet intervention in Afghanistan, and was perceived as a way to alleviate adversarial Indo-US relations. High-technology cooperation became the touchstone of Indo-US links, and was in many ways a confidence-building measure in that technology could be supplied to India without it slipping into Soviet hands or being used to build India's nuclear arsenal. It is not clear whether India shared this view, although it was willing to cooperate with the US on an international fissile-material-ban treaty and a comprehensive test-ban treaty as late as 1995 in return for access to conventional military high technology.[21]

As a result of this convergence of political and technological interests, India and the US embarked on high-technology co-operation during the 1980s. In 1986, the US Agency for International Development (USAID) began the Program for Acceleration of Commercial Technology (PACT) to promote joint ventures between private Indian and US companies developing new products and processes for commercial applications. The programme, modelled on the US–Israeli Bi-national Industry Research and Development (BIRD) programme, focused on pharmaceuticals, software and robotics.[22] According to one assessment, PACT has been a huge success, creating 47 joint ventures in fields such as information technology, chemical processes, energy and the environment, electrical and mechanical engineering and biotechnology.[23] In 1987, India and the US signed the Program for the Acceleration of Commercial Energy Research (PACER) to consider technical proposals to ease power shortages. The significance of this programme was twofold. First, it did not necessarily give India access to sensitive technology, but used bilateral aid to meet Indian energy needs. Second, it indicated US willingness to support India's public sector, which dominated energy production.[24] The overriding objective was to conduct research and development on a commercial basis.

The MOU Experience

The most significant agreement during this period was the Indo-US MOU signed in November 1984. This was crucial for two reasons. First, it related purely to defence technology, including dual technology, which, according to India, referred to items on the Commodities Control List (CCL), administered by the Department of Commerce, and the Munitions List, administered by the Department of State. In other words, it dealt with exports controlled by the US government for national-security as well as non-proliferation and foreign-policy purposes. Second, the MOU process, particularly the insistence on item-specific end-uses, especially for sensitive dual-use equipment, provided a forum in which to address proliferation issues.[25]

The objectives of the MOU were both political and technical. India aimed to accommodate US concerns regarding proliferation, while not compromising its stand against what it considered to be a discriminatory NPT regime. Senior Indian bureaucrats involved with the MOU point out that it was signed not only six years *after* the US NNPA was passed, but also without India's signature on the NPT.[26] In technological terms, India hoped that the MOU would reduce its dependence on Soviet military hardware by paving the way for continued and stable access to what was seen as superior technology from the US. According to one observer, the MOU was 'designed to reconcile India's weapons procurement policies with American technology transfer conditions and thereby expand military links'.[27] However, the technology-transfer phase of the MOU began only after a discernible Indian attempt to reassure the US that procedures had been established to ensure that the technology would neither leak to the Soviet Union nor be used for building nuclear weapons or missiles in India. India agreed:

> *To import the item into India and not to redirect it or any part of it, to another destination before its arrival in India ...*
> *To provide, if asked, verification that possession of the item was taken*
> *Not to re-export the item without the written approval of the Import Certificate Issuing Authority (ICIA), in India ...*
> *[and]*
> *Not to re-transfer within India the item(s) specified in this Certificate without the written approval of the ICIA.*[28]

In 1985, the US government decided to release General Electric's GE-404 engine for the LCA, and subsequently suggested that India consider a 'mission area' approach to defence-technology cooperation. This was an attempt to avoid time-consuming procedures in issuing export licences, particularly in agreed areas of cooperation. In February 1986, to assess the capability of India's defence laboratories and to identify areas in which the US could assist, the Deputy Director of the Defense Technology Security Administration, Talbot Lindstrom, visited New Delhi. His subsequent 50-page report became the basis for the evolution of the MOU. The report identified three potential areas for Indo-US defence cooperation. These were:

- aeronautics and aircraft technology in general, and the LCA in particular;
- third-generation anti-tank systems; and
- instrumentation and training for the National Test Range (NTR).[29]

Considerable progress was made in the first of these areas, particularly on the LCA. In early 1987, the US government prepared a *Blue Book* listing technologies that could be released to enable US industry to participate in the LCA programme. A Letter of Offer and Acceptance (LOA) under Foreign Military Sales (FMS) regulations was signed in September 1988, allowing India to use US government facilities and expertise, and to enable laboratory-to-laboratory cooperation in the aeronautics field. The two labs identified were the Wright-Patterson Air Force Laboratory in Ohio and the Aeronautical Development Establishment in Bangalore. Lab-to-lab cooperation led not only to technology transfer, but also to consultancy, training and visits to US government test-sites and industrial houses. According to one estimate, about $200m-worth of business has been conducted on the LCA project to date. When the LCA enters production early in the next century, this amount will increase.[30]

Despite this progress, in practice cooperation under the MOU and LOA was initially neither smooth nor trouble-free. The suspicions of Indian bureaucrats (who cited the 'betrayal' of the 1960s) was matched by the US military establishment's mistrust, particularly at the working level of the Department of Defense (DOD). Of the three services, the Navy was the most resistant to the National Security Decision Directives (NSDDs, pronounced 'nizdids') which sought enhanced cooperation. In addition, powerful non-proliferation purists in the Senate, such as John Glenn and Alan Cranston, were wary of increased technology transfer. A related factor was that, in the mid-1980s, some DOD officials were reluctant to expand security relations with India if doing so was likely to upset Pakistan. One State Department official recalled that the process of ensuring clearance and delivery of technology items was akin to 'trench warfare in World War I – slow and bloody'.[31]

Several problems did indeed emerge despite (or perhaps because of) the MOU provisions. These problems highlight the limitations of the MOU and the hurdles to future cooperation. There were three major areas of disagreement: the GE-404 engine for the LCA; the Cray XMP computer; and the radar and instrumentation for the NTR. Although the MOU and the Lindstrom visit should have cleared the way for the transfer of the GE-404, the engine was released only after Reagan's personal authorisation ended a fierce internal battle in the US government.[32] Similarly, the technical assistance that General Electric was to provide for an indigenous GE-404 upgrade, the *Kaveri* engine slated to power the LCA, was not forthcoming. Dr R. Krishnan, a former director of the Bangalore-based Gas Turbine Research Establishment (GTRE), builders of the *Kaveri*, revealed that the General Electric team made two visits to provide a detailed analysis of the engine as part of the LOA. While the first visit led to a detailed and 'good' technical report on the capabilities and, more significantly, the flaws of the *Kaveri*, the second yielded no such feedback. Krishnan felt that General Electric was 'prevented from presenting a report about the status of the *Kaveri* especially by the US Navy which probably regarded it as a competitor to the GE-404, which was then being considered for the F-18s'.[33]

If the MOU was the cake of Indo-US relations, the supply of the state-of-the-art Cray XMP-24 super-computer was to be the icing. India regarded supply of the Cray as a test of US credibility akin to Islamabad's perception of the supply of F-16 aircraft to Pakistan. New Delhi claimed that it wanted to use the computer to study the Indian monsoon. However, the machine's brute computing power also ideally suited it to nuclear-weapon and ballistic-missile development, as well as to deciphering cryptographic codes. The computer had only ever been sold to US allies, and the Indian request was regarded with deep suspicion by sections of the US government, which feared that New Delhi might use the Cray to move further down the proliferation path or – worse – share it with the Soviet Union, which had no comparable machine.[34] Debate in the US over the Cray saw the State and Commerce Departments in favour of the sale, with the Defense and Energy Departments and the National Security Agency (NSA) opposed. Finally, in March 1987, the Reagan administration reached a compromise: it would approve the sale of the Cray XMP-14 instead of the XMP-24. US experts argued that the XMP-14 could handle the weather-forecast work that India needed, but was incapable of cracking codes (the NSA's primary concern).[35] India was disappointed, but did not reject the offer outright; a group within the DRDO argued that it was essential to accept the computer to gain entry into the US high-technology world. Rajiv Gandhi agreed and approved the purchase of the XMP-14.[36] On a visit to the US in October 1987, Gandhi confirmed his decision to buy, and received an implicit US promise that it would provide additional computers to meet 'India's need for upgraded capability and the growing mutual confidence that the implementation of our agreement will provide'. Reagan also 'agreed to expand defence cooperation, proceeding along the lines we [India and the US] have already established in working together on aspects of the LCA, and in other areas'.[37]

A similar dispute arose over the Vitro 778 Instrumentation Radar for India's NTR. Both governments had cleared the radar's specifications under the MOU, and an export licence had been granted. However, the US Congress revoked the licence, then two years old, just a day before the radar was to be shipped out. This 'avoidable denial of items' caused India concern and renewed fears that, despite watertight assurances and a mutually agreed process, the US may be an unreliable technology supplier.[38]

By the end of the 1980s, it was clear that the MOU had not been an unqualified success. According to a senior DRDO bureaucrat, the MOU experience revealed that 'bids from US firms are invariably competitive, meet [specifications] and delivery schedules;

the MOU was not an unqualified success

but there is enormous delay ... in issue of export licences by [the US government] ... there is a big desire for more information in export licence processing; the info[rmation] loop is large, especially when multi-agency approval is required for a CCL item ... occasionally, there is a dilution of specifications ... occasionally, the licensing procedures do not reflect an awareness of technology'.[39]

These reservations notwithstanding, India acquired not only the GE-404 engine itself (which powered the F-15), but also the engine's technology and a new regime to cooperate on sub-components of the LCA. New Delhi also obtained LM-2500 gas-turbine engines for warships and the Cray XMP-14 super-computer. This was no mean achievement for two nations with virtually no history of such cooperation (aside from a brief period in the early 1960s), who harboured deep suspicions about each other's intentions and who were at loggerheads over the supply of nuclear fuel, the supply of arms to Pakistan and non-proliferation. It was, however, not surprising that technology transfer did not lead to technology cooperation or closer bilateral ties.

Factors That Limited Cooperation

Apart from the hurdles in the operation of the MOU that hindered greater strategic cooperation, several other factors limited Indo-US cooperation. First, the absence of a common strategic goal, especially after the end of the Cold War and the collapse of the Soviet Union, left no incentive for the Bush administration to woo India away from Moscow or even to accommodate it in its world view. The end of the Cold War left India without the 'Soviet card', especially as the Soviet military–industrial complex, which could have provided some of the technology that India sought at generous rates of exchange, was in disarray and incapable of providing equipment and technology even if it had wanted to. In addition, there was no clear indication from either the US or India of which potential threats would justify deeper strategic cooperation. Although the so-called 'Islamic threat' was raised in the media, it did not become a major issue. Similarly, although India had often raised the issue of China's supply of sensitive dual-use technology to Pakistan and Iran with the US, there was no official agreement or understanding between the two on how to deal with Beijing.

Second, slippage in Indian programmes, particularly the LCA, hampered Indo-US cooperation. This slippage was partly the result of managerial limitations, declining funding and inadequate planning (although one assessment attributes it also to the DRDO's inability to absorb the high technology it was importing).[40] Only in some cases could the delays be blamed on the US withholding technology.

Third, the coming of age of Pakistan's nuclear programme, and the Bush administration's inability to certify that Islamabad did not possess a nuclear device in 1990, appears to have had an adverse impact on India's nuclear self-restraint. India was likely to have seen defence-technology cooperation as part of a larger security package, which included US curtailment of Pakistan's nuclear-weapon capability. Perceived US leverage over Pakistan stemmed from Washington's supply of sophisticated conventional military aid. This aid was apparently conditional on Pakistan halting its nuclear-weapon programme. Rajiv Gandhi indicated India's perception of this leverage during his October 1987 visit to Washington, when he asserted: 'If the US really exerts pressure, I have no doubt that Pakistan will change its attitude towards the nuclear weapon programme.'[41] The inability of the US to ensure Pakistan's adherence to a non-nuclear status and to certify the absence of a nuclear-weapon capability would have been a major factor in India's decision to enhance its nuclear-weapon and delivery capability.

Fourth, a series of Indo-Pakistani crises during this period, which played themselves out in the subcontinent's emerging nuclear shadow, shaped Washington's view of the region's stability. In 1983–84 there were persistent reports of a possible Indian attack on Pakistan's nuclear-weapon production facilities, prompting Islamabad to threaten retaliatory strikes against Indian nuclear targets. India's *Brasstacks* exercise in 1986–87, its largest ever, took place close to the border, raising Pakistani fears that it would become an attack. Islamabad began a defensive deployment, *Operation Sledgehammer*, to which New Delhi responded with its own mobilisation. A crisis developed soon after Pakistan conducted its largest military exercise, *Zarb-i-Momin*, in late 1989. India rushed troops to Kashmir to counter growing pressure from militants there – a move seen as a hostile act by Pakistan, which threatened to weaponise its nuclear capability. Although neither India nor Pakistan possessed nuclear weapons, each period of tension certainly involved the nuclear-weapons card – the threat to build them; the threat to prevent their construction; and the threat to use them. This in turn prompted a tougher approach to regional proliferation from the Bush administration and from the first Clinton government.

Fifth, US non-proliferation purists staged a comeback during the Bush administration, especially in the wake of India's successful launch of the nuclear-capable *Agni* and *Prithvi* missiles and its quest for cryogenic engines, which the US feared could be used to power first-generation inter-continental ballistic missiles (ICBMs). Indian officials claim that they need cryogenic engines to launch heavier satellites into geo-synchronous orbits, and

from technology cooperation to sanctions

argue that no arsenal in the world contains cryogenically powered, nuclear-tipped missiles. US non-proliferation specialists, however, point out that US and Soviet first-generation ICBMs, such as the *Atlas, Thor,* SS-6 and SS-7, had cryogenic engines.[42] Thus, the emphasis shifted from technology cooperation to sanctions as a means to curb proliferation behaviour.

One victim was the $1.2m Combined Acceleration Vibration Climatic Test System (CAVCTS), the so-called 'shake-and-bake' rocket-testing device. The export of this sophisticated system, which simulated the heat and vibration of atmospheric re-entry, was reversed following the *Agni* test in 1989.[43] The Indian missile establishment compensated by building two separate devices (one to 'shake' and the other to 'bake'). Although the CAVCTS sanction may have delayed the missile programme, it did not curtail it, but forced India to develop an indigenous capability. Similarly, India's request for a more powerful super-computer, the Cray XMP-22, prompted unhappiness at the US DOD, Arms Control and Disarmament Agency (ACDA) and DOE, all of which suspected the machine's possible use in developing a nuclear-weapon capability. The sale of the computer was cleared only in December 1990 after the Bush administration negotiated supplementary controls to ensure that the Cray was not used to develop nuclear weapons. Again, India responded to US reluctance by striking out on its own, launching a programme to build a super-computer based on parallel computing.[44] India's quest for cryogenic engines from the Russian space agency *Glavkosmos* prompted a similar reaction from the US, which cited the MTCR and imposed a two-year ban on US contacts with both *Glavkosmos* and the ISRO. The $250m *Glavkosmos* deal was reduced to supplying seven cryogenic engines without technology transfer. Yet again, India elected to launch its own programme. In 1994, the ISRO began the Cryogenic Upper Stage (CUS) project, which aimed to accelerate the indigenous development of a cryogenic engine.

India's self-sufficient responses to sanctions not only prove them ineffective in the long term, but also raise the possibility that – should an indigenous capability in all these areas be successfully developed – India may become a supplier of these critical technologies. Although India has taken a status-quo stance towards the sale of dual-use technology, and has shown considerable restraint in supplying sensitive technology to other countries, New Delhi may be tempted not to do so in future, especially if the US exerts systematic pressure in the form of sanctions. If, on the other hand, Washington supplied the relevant technology as incentives with strict item-specific end-uses, or perhaps even reached a clear agreement that the technology is offered as part of a broader strategic deal, Indian technocrats may come round to Washington's way of thinking.

One of the biggest hurdles preventing closer cooperation is the difference in each country's perception of their technology relationship. For India, it is a five-tier pyramid, with technology transfer the base, followed by joint development, co-production, straight purchase of weapons and, at the apex, military-to-military cooperation. The US perception of the pyramid is the exact inverse.[45]

> **'the US is in a sell mode'**

Washington insists that strategic cooperation is the foundation of any relationship, with technology transfer at the top of the pyramid. A senior Pentagon official argued that one of the reasons for the slow progress in Indo-US technology cooperation is that 'the US is in a sell mode rather than a cooperation on research and development mode', and yet, 'US arms transfer comes with political baggage. There has to be some common strategic goal which does not exist at the moment between India and the US.'[46]

A Quid Pro Quo?

Has there ever been a concerted effort to identify common strategic goals? Were there attempts to reach an agreement – formal or informal – that India would give up or curb its nuclear option in exchange for US high technology, both nuclear and conventional? Did the US demand such a quid pro quo from India? Did India offer or agree to such an arrangement?

The historical evidence is equivocal at best. In early 1965, soon after the Chinese nuclear test, Dr Bhabha, India's atomic chief, told US Under-Secretary of State George Ball that 'a way must be found so that a nation will gain as much by not going for nuclear weapons as it might by developing them'.[47] Bhabha continued that 'ways must be found for it [India] to demonstrate to other Asian and African countries India's scientific achievements' – if its prestige was to be maintained in Chinese eyes.[48] The US responded by sending Dr Jerome Weisner, a government scientific adviser, to New Delhi to help India to 'demonstrate that its scientific and technical capabilities are at least equal to those of Chicoms [Chinese Communists]'.[49] Weisner was to 'reinforce the Indian decision [to] stick to its current nuclear policy' and to 'draw Indian leaders into serious talks on [the] dangers and implications of nuclear proliferation'.[50] Weisner's lack of a firm mandate may have led the Indian leadership to believe that this was not a serious proposal, and no agreement was reached. Moreover, as the discussions also covered the possible peaceful uses of nuclear energy, particularly the role of the US *Plowshare* programme in 'making harbours and water reservoirs' in India, Indian officials may have assumed that the US was endorsing 'peaceful nuclear explosions'.[51]

In 1970, the US made explicit that it 'would not consider the use of plutonium produced in the CIRUS reactor for peaceful nuclear explosives intended for any purpose to be research into and use of atomic energy for peaceful purposes'.[52] The Indian response – if one was forthcoming – is unclear. What is certain is that India conducted a nuclear test on 18 May 1974 using plutonium from CIRUS.

In the early 1980s, there is evidence to suggest that Indira Gandhi reached an understanding with the US that India would refrain from further tests. According to one report, a senior MEA official assured the US State Department's Officer-in-Charge of Proliferation, James Malone, that India would not conduct a 'PNE [peaceful nuclear explosion] in a current time frame'.[53] Again, this was a tacit understanding which seems to have ended in 1983, when India perceived that the US was unable to curtail Pakistan's programme and thus prepared to conduct a nuclear test (none took place).[54]

In the 1990s, another quid pro quo was mooted at a semi-formal meeting between senior Indian and US officials. Under this proposal, India sought a waiver under the 1978 NNPA to ensure continued contractual supply of low-enriched uranium for the

Tarapur nuclear reactor; the removal of the Polar, Geosynchronous and Augmented SLVs and the *Prithvi* from Supplement 6 to Part 778 of the Export Administration Regulations (EAR); and a meaningful reduction in pre-licence checks and post-shipment verification of some sensitive high technology originally visualised in the MOU. In return, India was willing to cooperate in formulating and piloting through negotiations an international treaty halting production of fissile material for weapons; a non-discriminatory CTBT; preparing a core list of proliferation-sensitive items for inclusion in India's export-control regulations; and adopting 'non-weaponised' or 'recessed' nuclear deterrence in line with multilateral and international moves towards a non-discriminatory, verifiable regime.[55] However, India's subsequent stance on the CTBT revealed that even this nebulous understanding was transient. In May 1997, at a similar seminar organised by the University of Pennsylvania, US and Indian officials discussed the possibility of a 'deal' in which Washington would amend its nuclear legislation to help India with civilian nuclear-power generation and lift controls on technology transfer if India agreed to 'formalise its nuclear restraint' and not conduct any nuclear explosions.[56] This semi-official proposal, although it has not been formally followed up, indicates both sides' desire to continue dialogue to define areas of mutual interest and to attempt cooperation in these areas. This has led both sides to seek new avenues and models of interaction, as well as to revive, improve and enlarge the MOU. The vehicles used by the LCA-programme participants, particularly the LOA mechanism under which even sensitive technology transfer was facilitated, have now been employed in several other projects. Since this is a tried-and-tested process, it has the potential to oil the wheels of future cooperation, and could become an important component of a strategic relationship.

chapter 3

Prospects for Indo-US Strategic Cooperation

The prospects for Indo-US strategic cooperation depend primarily on both countries' success in ensuring their security and prestige and satisfying their domestic technological and political imperatives. Finding common ground on the strategic future is one way in which New Delhi and Washington will be able to ensure Indian security. In the post-Cold War world, it is not clear where this common ground may lie, although some US analysts have suggested that a 'strong and friendly India could help maintain stability and prosperity throughout Asia'.[1] Others say that it would be in the interests of the US to strengthen India as a bulwark against possible instability in China and the Persian Gulf, and to increase US economic investment in India.[2] It may be in India's interests to use US influence at the World Trade Organisation (WTO) to ensure that China's entry does not weaken its position.[3] It is not clear whether there is consensus in India on these views: having pursued a relatively independent foreign policy since the end of the Raj, New Delhi may not be keen to work too closely with Washington either in the region or in global organisations.

Economic relations appear to be the one area in which there is consensus, despite a history of serious disputes. These include differences over the Special 301 provisions of the US Congress' 1988 Omnibus Trade and Competitiveness Act (popularly known as the 'Super 301'); India remains on the Act's priority watch-list. In the early 1990s, India was reluctant to adhere to the international convention on intellectual property rights, especially in pharma-ceuticals.[4] Substantial Indo-US disagreements have emerged in the WTO with regard to patent protection and Quantitative Restrictions (QRs).[5] In the face of these differences – and several changes of government, including some with members from communist parties – India's economic reforms have remained on track and investment by US companies has continued. Despite Enron's difficulties with the Maharashtra state government over its proposed Dabhol project, the company has not pulled out – and may set up more power plants.[6] Similarly, demonstrations against a Kentucky Fried Chicken (KFC) outlet in Bangalore in 1997 have not prompted KFC to abandon its plans to expand in India. This is not altruism but a recognition of the commercial opportunities provided by the sheer size of the Indian market.[7] The cost of adding 100,000MW of generating capacity, 13,000km of roads, 200m tonnes of cargo-handling port capacity and 60m telephone lines over the next decade is estimated at $200bn.[8] India's public and private sector can raise only a third of this amount. If New Delhi can ensure adequate returns on investment, as it did in Enron's case, India promises to be an investor's paradise.

Recognition of India's Strategic Status

To ensure that the prestige factor behind India's nuclear drive is satisfied, the only acceptable incentive for India to reconsider its traditional position on proliferation would perhaps be the *de facto* recognition of its legitimate national-security interests. A corollary might mean accepting India's nuclear-weapon capability. A degree of tacit recognition is already in place: during the CTBT negotiations, India, along with Israel and Pakistan, was referred to as a 'threshold nuclear state'. A more explicit recognition of India's nuclear-weapon capability would not be necessary, particularly since New Delhi regards it more in political and prestige, rather than military, terms. This support could be implicit in, for example, US backing for India's candidacy for UNSC membership. Such a deal would resemble the 'opening' made by the US towards mainland China in 1971–72 which led to the engagement and eventual recognition of the Beijing government in 1979. The parallel between the US opening to China and current US relations with India is clear, even though it was easier to recognise Beijing's nuclear arsenal as it conducted its test before the NPT's 1968 cut-off date and was recognised as a nuclear-weapon state under the Treaty. Not recognising India's current nuclear status would possibly provide a rationale for Indian hawks to proliferate further on the grounds that the US recognised China because Beijing possessed nuclear weapons. As a logical corollary, so the hawks argue, the US will not recognise India's nuclear position unless New Delhi has nuclear weapons. US backing for Indian UNSC hopes is likely only if the current situation – where the five permanent members are also the five recognised nuclear-weapon states – changes. This may happen since the US has supported the entry of Germany and Japan onto the Council, neither of which is a nuclear-weapon state.

An Indo-US agreement along the lines of backing for UNSC membership and recognition of India's nuclear status would go a long way to satisfying India's security concerns and meeting its prestige and domestic-technological imperatives. In return, India would need to continue its self-imposed freeze on developing its nuclear-weapon capabilities. By accepting India's current nuclear posture, the US would effectively achieve its twin purpose of preventing overt proliferation in South Asia and ensuring that nuclear-weapon technology is not transferred to other potentially proliferating regions. A closer strategic engagement would also facilitate locking India into multilateral non-proliferation agreements such as the NSG and the MTCR.

Resolving security and prestige issues would pave the way for technology cooperation, particularly dual-use technology. This would be essential to ensure that the talents of India's nuclear and missile scientists, a crucial impetus for any weapons of mass destruction (WMD) programme, can be channelled in non-weapon directions. This is, however, easier said than done given the two sides' diametrically opposed perceptions of the cooperation model, particularly in high-technology defence. India is willing to begin with technology transfer and progress towards military-to-military cooperation within a strategic partnership. For the US, however, the starting point would have to be a strategic and military partnership eventually leading to technology transfer and cooperation.

Potential Areas of Cooperation

Given these considerations, there are three crucial high-technology areas in which India seeks cooperation with the US: defence and security; space; and energy. Cooperation in the defence, security and nuclear-energy fields is clearly the most important as it deals directly with proliferation and prestige issues. Given both sides' desire to find common ground to enable cooperation, it is important to examine the areas in which links already exist. There are currently three such areas: conventional-defence research and development (R&D) and technology transfer, including dual-use technology; military-to-military cooperation, including joint exercises and, possibly, equipment purchases; and work towards establishing shared objectives such as the CTBT and common regional security goals.

Cooperation in Defence

There have been attempts in the 1990s to formalise and widen cooperation between the defence establishments of the two countries based on the experiences of the 1980s, particularly through the 1984 MOU. These efforts reflect not only the nature of Indo-US links, but also of the internal debate between constituents in both countries. For example, the MOU and the 1987 Mission Area of Cooperation were essentially driven by the civilian-dominated DRDO in a bid not only to acquire the necessary technology from the US, but also to monopolise the relationship at the expense of the armed forces. The military, which was keen to establish its own links with its US counterpart, found itself effectively sidelined.

As a result, there was an attempt in 1991 to establish service-to-service cooperation. This effort was initiated by General Claude M. Kicklighter, the former Commandant of the US Army Pacific Command (USAPAC), during a visit to India in November 1991. Joint Steering Committees (JSCs) were set up to allow each country's armed services to coordinate personnel exchanges, joint training and exercises and information-sharing. This was in keeping with the US desire to promote military-to-military cooperation initially, but not to transfer technology in the first instance. Technology transfer was to be dependent on the nature and extent of cooperation. US Joint Chief of Staff General Colin Powell in December 1992 told the then Indian Ambassador to the US, Siddharth Shankar Ray, that 'a strong and secure bridge must be built before too many vehicles are put on it'.[9] For the same reason, this initiative was not supported by India's civilian-led DRDO and MOD, which wanted technology transfer rather than military-to-military cooperation to be the basis of the Indo-US relationship, even though it was enthusiastically welcomed by the three armed services. The civilians won the day, and the Kicklighter proposals never really took off. The next significant step in defence cooperation was taken following the US visit of then Indian Prime Minister Rao in May 1994, when the two sides agreed to closer defence cooperation.

Rao's visit was followed in January 1995 by the signing of the first-ever agreed minutes on Indo-US defence cooperation by then US Secretary of Defense William Perry. This became the umbrella arrangement for earlier agreements, particularly the 1984 MOU and the Kicklighter joint-exercise proposal. Under the agreed minutes, cooperation expanded between India's MOD and its US counterpart; the Indian and US militaries; and the DRDO and US defence R&D and production sectors. The Perry initiative was successful primarily because it satisfied the concerns of both the civilian and military constituents of the US and Indian defence establishments. The civilians were satisfied that they could keep a check on the military. The armed forces were content with direct contact with the US military and with joint exercises. The DRDO was happy that the Perry initiative not only retained the level of cooperation agreed under the MOU, but also formalised and expanded it.

Three separate bodies were established to facilitate discussion and interaction: the Defence Policy Group (DPG); the Joint Technical Group (JTG); and modified versions of the earlier JSCs. The DPG, which comprised civilian bureaucrats from the MOD and the MEA, became the first among equals, primarily because its members outranked those of the other groups. The DPG was authorised to discuss not only defence issues, but also subjects such as the CTBT and Kashmir. The modified JSCs continued the work of their predecessors, discussing personnel and information exchange, as

well as joint exercises. The JTG, which comprised defence technocrats, was to discuss defence-research issues.

For the purposes of technology cooperation, the JTG is the
most significant of the three bodies. It was devised as the senior
bilateral forum in which the US and Indian defence departments
could discuss and coordinate research and development, production, procurement and logistics. Its goal was to establish a
framework for bilateral technology cooperation, to monitor progress
and to provide a forum in which the policies, plans and
requirements of both sides could be aired. The JTG's first meeting
was held, along with that of the DPG, in September 1995. A range of
topics was discussed, including technology transfer and cooperation, equipment-testing and evaluation, simulation and war-
gaming, software engineering, 'COTS' (commercial off-the-shelf)
philosophy, non-lethal technology and defence management. The
participants narrowed the agenda for the second DPG/JTG meeting
in October 1996 to test and evaluation, simulation, flight and
armoured vehicles and naval systems.[10] A third meeting was
scheduled for late 1997. Its objective, according to one JTG member,
was to assess what the Indians were looking for, particularly in test
and evaluation, and the possibility of a separate test-and-evaluation
directorate within the DRDO. Non-lethal technology, particularly for
riot control, was also to be on the agenda. India is keen to discuss a
possible joint programme for unmanned aerial vehicles (UAVs) and
JTG help in selling some DRDO equipment, such as bridge-layers, to
the US military. Technical cooperation has not been confined to the
annual JTG/DPG meetings. For example, three military attachés and
the DRDO representative in Washington, led by the Indian Ambassador, visited US Central Command headquarters in Florida and
Pacific Command HQ in Hawaii in 1994, ensuring that cooperation
is a continuous process.

A close evaluation of the JTG reveals several interesting
trends. The basis it envisages for technology transfer remains the
MOU, both in form and content. The JTG's focus on flight vehicles
and test-and-evaluation equipment is a continuation of the MOU,
which stressed cooperation in aeronautics and aircraft technology,
third-generation anti-tank systems and instrumentation and training
for the NTR. Although the JTG has superseded the MOU, the focus

remains the same. There are also indications that India would like to expand technology cooperation to include armoured vehicles and naval systems, and to include UAVs in the aeronautics category. Under the MOU, transfer was confined to night-vision devices for armoured vehicles, engines for naval ships and aeronautical systems for the LCA. Thus, the JTG appears to start where the MOU left off.

There are several reasons why India stresses the MOU process as the basis for continuing interaction with the US. First, despite several drawbacks, it was an accepted and successful instrument in significantly increasing Indo-US sensitive-technology trade during the 1980s. At the same time, it alleviated US proliferation concerns. Second, the higher-level assurances negotiated under the MOU, which appeared to address US concerns, to a substantial degree remain relevant – even in the post-Cold War era. Third, new concerns, particularly regarding pro-liferation, are still likely to be best tackled under the MOU. Creating a new framework would be time-consuming. The MOU was also con-

India stresses the MOU process

sidered a 'constructive sub-set of the larger set of initiatives in evolving bilateral cooperation between India and the US'.[11] The MOU process was seen as the path of least resistance, where serious disagreement between India and the US was unlikely. Technology cooperation under the JTG in tandem with the DPG is also seen as an important means by which both parties can engage with the other side's decision-makers, particularly those with a role in nuclear and defence policy.

The engagement process, which began in 1994–95 when India indicated that it would cooperate with the US on the CTBT, continued despite India's later block on the Treaty. Engagement was made possible by the DPG's focus, which tried to explore common security perspectives beyond a narrow emphasis on the proliferation issue. These perspectives included possible efforts to counter China and to improve stability in the region and in the Persian Gulf. The DPG also provided the ideal medium in which to discuss India's security concerns, such as Kashmir. This was crucial since strategic cooperation is possible only when a common goal has been identified. Although there is no consensus on which, if any, common strategic interest could bring about Indo-US cooperation, the DPG has provided the forum in which the issue can at least be discussed.

The DPG process has also offered a means of private communication on subjects over which the two sides are publicly at loggerheads. This is not to say that this process is beyond the purview of the Indian parliament or the US Congress, merely that it offers an opportunity to thrash out issues which would not otherwise be discussed. Although neither side has been able to change the other's mind, interaction through this medium has certainly had an impact on US decision-makers' perceptions. It is therefore crucial that they keep talking.

Cooperation in Space

Space research may be another area of possible Indo-US cooperation. The US has worked with China and Russia in this area as a means of enhancing technology cooperation and influencing proliferation behaviour. In a bid to prevent Russia from supplying cryogenic-engine technology to India, the US offered Moscow extensive cooperation in three areas: joint scientific research involving the US space shuttle and Russia's *Mir* space station; Russian partnership in the International Space Station; and a trade agreement on Russian commercial launch services.[12] Similar deals were also approved for China in 1988.[13]

Space cooperation can be divided into two distinct categories: the launch segment; and the space-applications segment. The former is sensitive because it deals with rocket technology which could be used for military missiles. It is also lucrative, accounting for the large profits of the space agencies. The latter includes processing and disseminating satellite data and other services, most of which are ground-based and use the data provided by an orbiting satellite. This includes downloading and interpreting data for remote-sensing, providing receiving and transmitting stations for satellites and leasing out satellite transponders. These applications, such as broadcasting, telecommunications and remote-sensing, tend to be less sensitive than the launch segment, with a longer pay-back period and smaller profit margins.[14] A further distinction in space cooperation – that between commercial and non-commercial links – is also relevant. The first refers to business deals between space organisations, both government and private, driven by profit. The second may deal in the same area, but is generally a government-to-government agreement which is not usually designed to make a profit.

Given that access to the launch market is considered particularly sensitive, the US is unlikely to open it to India. Administration officials feel that to do so could subsidise India's missile programme and boost proliferation. This perception was reinforced in the wake of the US decision to allow Chinese entry into the launch market in 1988.[15] Washington was subsequently unable to control Beijing's proliferation behaviour. US space companies, which had agreed to use Chinese launchers, put pressure on Washington not to impose sanctions for fear that they would affect business.[16] Moreover, India's launch capability has yet to establish a proven track record and customers are unlikely to flock to the ISRO, despite a competitive launch price of $70m. In the long term, India may be able to carve itself a launch-market niche once it perfects a reliable and economical launch vehicle, particularly its Polar SLV, which is similar to the Russian *Molniya*-class launcher. In the short term, however, all that New Delhi can hope for is to launch its own satellites, thereby saving foreign exchange.

Cooperation in the space-application segment, particularly with regard to global services such as weather forecasting and telecommunications, is less controversial because the risk of proliferation is low and its benefits are seen to be in the interest of all mankind. Perhaps for these reasons, the history of Indo-US cooperation in space applications stretches back to 1963, and has continued through the stormiest phases in their relations. Cooperation in this field is therefore likely to face the least resistance within India and the US.

Until the 1990s, foreign exchange to pay for space services, including launches, data-purchases and the use of satellites, flowed almost exclusively from India to the US. However, following the creation of Antarix, the marketing arm of the ISRO, and the growth of indigenous technology and expertise in space applications, particularly in the remote-sensing field, the foreign-exchange relationship has become less one-sided. In the mid-1990s, Indo-US space cooperation has taken two forms:

- *Government-to-government*: between NASA and the ISRO, as well as between India's Department of Science and Technology (DST), particularly its meteorology department, and NASA and the US National Oceanic and Atmospheric Administration (NOAA).
- *Commercial*: for example, a deal between the US company Space Imaging Eosat and Antarix to market Indian Remote Sensing (IRS) satellite data world-wide.

As both these areas are of mutual interest and came into being after prolonged negotiations, they hold the key to future cooperation and are worth examining in detail. This study should be seen against the backdrop of the proliferation issue to assess whether these agreements were incentives to non-proliferation, or whether they were driven by commercial considerations and emerged despite proliferation concerns.

The Space Imaging Eosat–Antarix deal was born in the 1980s, when the US government decided to commercialise the sale of *Landsat* images in a bid to make its land remote-sensing programme self-sustaining and independent of government funding. Eosat of Lanham (Maryland) was created to market the *Landsat* images. Neither NASA nor the US government was directly involved in establishing Eosat, although the organisation was allowed to use the ground-station at Norman (Oklahoma), which was part of the *Landsat* programme. One of Eosat's earliest customers was the ISRO, which bought *Landsat* images to supplement those it received from its IRS-1A and 1B satellites. The ISRO's ground-station at Shadnagar received these images, which were used by a variety of Indian customers, including the Forestry Department. In 1990, Eosat asked the ISRO whether it would be interested in selling its IRS images globally. The ISRO felt that it did not have the skills to market the images, and in 1992 entered negotiations with Eosat and France's *SPOT*, the other serious competitor to the IRS-1C.

Eosat was particularly keen on the IRS-1C, which was launched in December 1995. Its imagery was considered complementary to that of *Landsat*, and would thus enhance Eosat's portfolio. A deal with the ISRO became even more attractive when, in September 1993, the improved *Landsat* 6, which was to replace the

Figure 1 *IRS Satellite Constellation*

Satellite	Launch	Instruments	Spatial Resolution	Swath	Geographic Coverage	Repeat Coverage
IRS-1A	1989	LISS-1 Multispectral LISS-2 Multispectral	72.5m 36.25m	148km 74km	Decommissioned	22 days
IRS-1B	1991	LISS-1 Multispectral LISS-2 Multispectral	72.5m 36.25m	148km 74km	Shadnagar/Norman	22 days
IRS-P2	1994	LISS-2 Multispectral	32x37m	67km	Shadnagar/Norman	24 days
IRS-1C	1995	LISS-3 Multispectral WiFS Wide-Field Panchromatic	23.5M VNIR 70.5M SWIR 188m 5.8m	142km 148km 774km 70km	8 IGSs by 1996 plus on-board tape recorders	24 days 5 days 5 days
IRS-P3	1996	MOS-A MOS-B MOS-C WiFS X-ray Astronomy Payload	2.5x2.5m 720x580m 1x.7km 188m	248km 248km 248km 774km	Shadnagar/Norman/ Neustrelitz	– – – 5 days
IRS-P4	1996	Ocean Sensor LISS-3 Multispectral or Panchromatic				
IRS-P5	1997	MAPSat fore/aft Stereo				
IRS-P6	1998	Environmental				
IRS-1D	1999	LISS-3 Multispectral WiFS Wide-Field Panchromatic	23.5M VNIR 70.5M SWIR 188m <10m	142km 148km 774km 70km		24 days 5 days 5 days

Source: Eosat

Map 4 *IRS-1C Ground Receiving Stations*

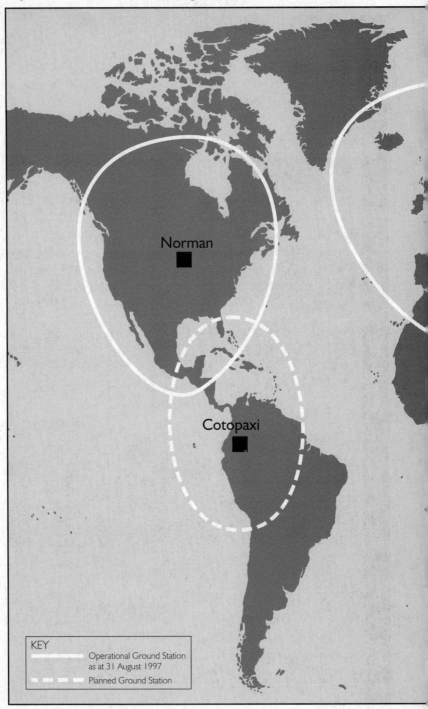

KEY

Operational Ground Station
as at 31 August 1997

Planned Ground Station

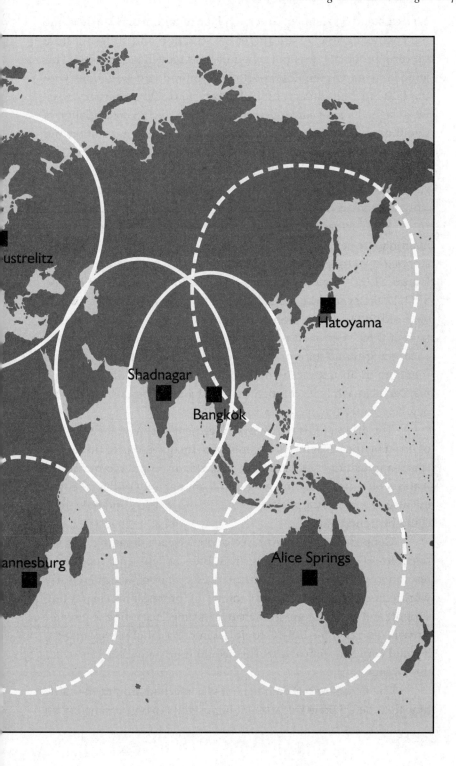

Landsat 4 and 5 satellites, suffered a launch failure and crashed into the Pacific. *Landsat* 7, still under construction and suffering from funding problems, was not scheduled for launch before 1998. This left a large gap in the Eosat portfolio, prompting negotiations with the ISRO to begin in earnest in January 1994. On 4 February 1995, Eosat signed a ten-year agreement to market the IRS constellation of satellites world-wide, share access fees for each ground-station and pay the ISRO a 10% royalty on its data sales. According to one estimate, India could earn about $100m from the deal.[17] Some reports suggest that in its first year of operation, IRS-1C is expected to net close to $10m in foreign exchange.[18]

SPOT setbacks further strengthened India's position. France's main remote-sensing satellite, the three-year-old *SPOT* 3, suddenly stopped operating in 1996. According to *Space News*, France cannot launch *SPOT* 4 before late 1997 or early 1998, and has to rely on *SPOT* 2 (a seven-year-old satellite). France is reactivating the 11-year-old *SPOT* 1 as a stop-gap. At the same time, India plans to launch three improved remote-sensing satellites by 1999 and, by 1998, ten ground-stations are expected to be operational. India is therefore in an unprecedented position to progress in securing a market niche while its competitors are at a disadvantage and before new ones enter the market in 1997–98.[19]

The original Eosat–Antarix agreement survived the takeover of Eosat by the US aerospace giant Space Imaging, one of the largest space-application companies in the US, in 1997. According to Antarix officials, Space Imaging told them not only of the takeover, but also of some of the glitches in the IRS-1C imagery and how these could be ironed out.[20]

Cooperation with Antarix offered Space Imaging a wide portfolio of products, ranging from one- to ten- and 100-metre-resolution satellite imagery. For Antarix, its product, which is clearly world-class, now has the advantage of professional marketing support and assured foreign-exchange income. According to a senior Antarix official, if the IRS-1C could eat into the aerial survey market, it could earn $20–30m a year. This would fund a new satellite every three years.

The Eosat–Antarix agreement was reached around the same time that the US State Department imposed its two-year sanction on

Glavkosmos and the ISRO over the cryogenic-engine deal.[21] Some senior US officials asserted that the IRS-1C deal was a deliberate bid to influence India's proliferation behaviour.[22] If so, it did not have the desired effect: in 1994 India conducted its third *Agni* test.[23] Even if the deal was a non-proliferation incentive, it was neither spelt out as such by either government, nor did Antarix or Eosat consider this to be the case. For example, senior Indian officials involved are categoric that 'this was a private deal. There was no US government involvement at all. It had no relation to the cryogenic deal.'[24] By the same token, Space Imaging officials wanted to keep the government informed but not involved. However, the US government's important role in setting up Eosat (by providing its ground-station), and its awareness of the IRS-1C deal, may have led Washington to believe that it was indeed offering an incentive, even though it was not perceived as such.

Lisa Shaffer, Director of the Mission to Planet Earth division of NASA's Office of External Relations, endorses the non-incentive view, arguing that 'NASA does not interfere with US companies reaching agreements with the ISRO. We just want to protect our technical expertise.'[25] But the US government's two-year sanction virtually froze contacts between NASA and the ISRO and was influenced by the administration's non-proliferation concerns. This action appears to have harmed NASA more than the ISRO. For years, NASA had been trying to gain access to the weather data collected *the US two-year sanction* by the ISRO's *INSAT* satellites as part of its global weather-study project. NASA wanted direct access to India's data almost immediately after it was collected by the spacecraft. However, India was reluctant to part with this data, which related exclusively to the subcontinent, and was of potential strategic value to India's adversaries, particularly Pakistan. In addition, making this data available would have necessitated a direct telecom link with the Indian Meteorological Department.[26] Just when there were indications that India, which was keen to participate in several global space- and earth-science programmes, was willing to part with the data as a quid pro quo, the US imposed its two-year sanction. This delayed a potential partnership which would have benefited both the ISRO and NASA.

ISRO–NASA negotiations over data-sharing restarted in earnest in 1995, when ISRO chief K. Kasturirangan offered NASA the *INSAT* data. A statement of intent was drawn up in the wake of a US delegation's visit to India in 1996, in which India not only offered to make the *INSAT* data available to the US government, but also to establish a communications link over which it could be transmitted digitally. In return, India would gain access to US environmental data as well as the chance of participating in programmes such as Mission to Planet Earth. The agreement was expected to be signed in late 1997. According to Shaffer 'we've held out *INSAT* data as a necessary step they have to take before we'll talk about [cooperating on] anything else'.[27] Again, there are indications that this hard bargain was not an incentive to influence Indian proliferation behaviour, but simply a tactic to reach the most advantageous cooperative agreement. While the *INSAT* deal would have been impossible had the proliferation-related ban not been lifted, it also appears that NASA's desire to cooperate with the ISRO is not dictated purely by proliferation concerns. Thus, as soon as the ban was lifted, NASA and the ISRO sought a mutually acceptable agreement which is now on the verge of signature. In addition, the ISRO has outlined an ambitious plan (*Proposals and Cooperation with NASA and NOAA in Space, Meteorology and Atmospheric Sciences*) to expand areas of cooperation.

Cooperation in Energy

India produced 365kWh of electricity per capita in 1991–92; the US produced 533kWh per capita in 1920, revealing India's desperate need to boost its energy production and improve transmission. India has an installed capacity of 83,000MW and intends to add another 57,000MW in coming years. However, it lacks the capital and, in some cases, the technology to meet this target. There is therefore enormous potential for Indo-US cooperation in this area. Such cooperation can be divided into nuclear and non-nuclear categories. Non-nuclear would in particular include thermal, hydroelectric and gas (power plants based on alternative sources, such as wind and solar energy, have yet to be built on a commercially viable scale).

India needs capital and technology

Of the country's 83,000MW installed capacity, nuclear power accounts for 0.3% of India's total commercial power output (coal accounts for around 60%, petroleum 27%, natural gas 8% and hydro 3%).[28] According to parliament's Standing Committee on Energy, nuclear's meagre share is the result of the government's *'ad hoc'* approach to India's nuclear-power programme. The Committee pointed out that an ambitious plan launched in 1984 to install 10,000MW of nuclear power by 2000 was scaled down to 3,320MW by 2004. Indian scientists claim that this was the result of inadequate funds rather than lack of technical ability, but the Committee pointed out that critical items for the plants, which were bought in advance at a cost of R136.6m ($3.9m), remained unused.[29] A recent report suggests that the Indian nuclear-power programme, based on the three-phase plan outlined by Bhabha in 1954, is constrained by the inability to construct adequate pressurised heavy water reactors (PHWRs), the limited supply of domestic uranium and the non-viability of fast-breeder reactors.[30] These drawbacks may explain India's desire to cooperate with the US in the nuclear sphere. Despite international statistics proving otherwise, New Delhi regards nuclear power as cost-effective; the country's nuclear programme is well rounded and India's technicians have extensive experience in building power plants and a long history of cooperation with their US counterparts.

However, following the NPT in 1968, India's 1974 nuclear test, the 1978 US NNPA and the creation of the NSG, the Indian and US positions became intractable. Washington insists on complete nuclear safeguards at all facilities as the basis for future cooperation; New Delhi is equally adamant that blanket safeguards are discriminatory and out of the question. Progress in this area is therefore particularly problematic. Over the last few years, however, India has softened its stance, making several suggestions ranging from accepting international safeguards at its power reactors (but not its research reactors, which house the weapon capability) to the concept of 'island' safeguards. This idea envisages establishing 100% foreign-owned reactors 'islanded' (i.e., separated) from India's nuclear programme and therefore governed by different rules.[31] Another alternative has been to look for suppliers of natural uranium which do not insist on comprehensive safeguards to fuel the Tarapur and other reactors. India points out that this is based on the original arrangement with the US under which Washington promised to supply uranium for Tarapur. Subsequently, a trilateral fuel-supply agreement was established between France, India and the IAEA. China has also undertaken to supply uranium for Tarapur under an India–China–IAEA arrangement. Although the Indians point to this process as a model of cooperation for other nuclear powers, there have as yet been no takers.

In the absence of substantial progress on the nuclear-power front, other energy sources, particularly gas, thermal and hydro, may offer greater prospects for cooperation. Enron's arrival in India is to some extent evidence of the possibilities in the gas-powered area. However, natural gas is not available in sufficient quantities domestically. To tap resources beyond its boundaries, India and the US would have to lay pipelines through the territory of potential adversaries, such as Pakistan and Iran, or through politically un-stable regions such as Central Asia. An alternative being examined is to buy surplus power from neighbouring countries, notably Pakistan. By unifying their power hubs, India could partly cover its shortfall of over 16,600MW.[32] Setting up a synchronous Indo-Pakistani grid system is technically feasible and appropriate measures can ensure compatibility (as between the US and Canada).

The 'Privatised' Relationship

India's economic reforms and the Clinton administration's relaxation of export controls, particularly on computers (among the most contentious export items in the 1980s), have made exclusive Indo-US government-to-government agreements appear redundant. High-technology transfer has shrunk dramatically, to be replaced by increased commercial cooperation in all spheres, especially space research and computing. According to one US scholar, 'the Indo-US relationship has now been privatised'.[33]

This 'privatised relationship' could generate its own com-petition and conflict, and does not necessarily guarantee trouble-free association – as is apparent in the current tussle between India and the US over Quantitative Restrictions. In addition, economic and commercial cooperation is only one aspect of the overall strategic relationship between India and the US. It cannot drive other elements of the relationship, particularly those related to security and high technology, both of which are still determined by governments.

India and the US share government-to-government links in defence and security; partly official association in the space sphere; and a commercial relationship in the energy sector. This allows for contacts which will determine the pace and extent of future Indo-US cooperation.

A Snail-paced Partnership?

Were India's ideal wish-list to come true, the country would be recognised as enjoying the rights accorded to a legitimate nuclear-weapon state: possessing nuclear weapons and conducting a nuclear-weapon programme; a seat on the UNSC; and importing nuclear material and power plants free from full-scope safeguards. This is, however, wishful thinking, even though India has already fulfilled the duties of a nuclear-weapon state by ensuring that its nuclear-weapon technology is not passed to other countries. To some extent India (along with Israel and Pakistan) has been recognised as a 'threshold' nuclear power during the course of the CTBT negotiations. However, none of the rights of a nuclear-weapon state has been bestowed on any of the three, nor are they likely to be.

India's nuclear-weapon capability is more likely to be recognised – and the country accorded special status – if it does not exercise this option. This is not unprecedented: both Germany and Japan have developed advanced indigenous nuclear technology which makes them capable of manufacturing nuclear weapons. Their technological capability has been accepted on the understanding that they do not weaponise it. Locking both countries into multilateral non-proliferation regimes such as the NPT has legitimised this arrangement. Granted, both countries have been accorded this special status because of their strategic alliance with the US, and on the strict understanding that Washington would guarantee their security with a nuclear umbrella.

While India is unwilling to accept, and unlikely to expect, an external nuclear guarantee, it is likely to keep its nuclear-weapon option in abeyance as long as its right to maintain and exercise the weapon option in the national-security interest is recognised. Indian strategists have often expressed this view; the country's official strategist, Jasjit Singh, argued:

> *Countries like Canada, Sweden, Japan, Germany, Switzer-land, Belgium and India ... do not have a weapons programme. But the technological base is more than adequate to achieve weaponisation at short notice. On the other hand they may never cross the threshold of weapon-isation. This level of capability provides the states with a recessed deterrent – which need not surface at all, but capability of which will have to be taken into account by any power contemplating using threat of nuclear coercion or weapons.*[1]

Although New Delhi and Washington have often discussed India's nuclear capability, there has never been a formal quid pro quo along the German or Japanese model – acceptance of India's legitimate nuclear capability with the explicit understanding that the inherent weapon capability would not be exercised unless national security was threatened. Both sides have tried

a trend towards mutual accommodation

to address this issue several times, but no explicit agreement has been reached. At best, there appear to have been periods of short-lived mutual understanding. This suggests, however, a trend towards mutual accommodation and a desire to reach an equitable and formal agreement on the nuclear issue. This has in the past been impossible for a variety of reasons: the Cold War and India's perceived tilt towards the Soviet Union; the US attempt to accommodate China and Pakistan; India's insulated market and mixed-economy model, with its emphasis on centrally planned enterprises; and the ideological foreign-policy approach of both the US and India, particularly over the nuclear issue.

A tacit acceptance of the Indian position – with or without nuclear guarantees – is likely only if India and the US share strategic interests. As the preceding chapters have shown, mutual interests have emerged in the political, economic, strategic and proliferation spheres in the post-Cold War era. India's economic reforms and its desire to throw open its markets to global competition, its pragmatic approach to foreign policy, its commitment to curbing terrorism and the drugs trade, as well as limiting WMD proliferation and protecting the environment, are similar to the approach adopted by the US.

According to one estimate, India's GDP ranks fifth on a purchasing-power-parity basis (after the US, China, Japan and Germany).[2] Economic expert Jeffrey Sachs has argued that it is in the interest of the Group of Seven (G-7) advanced industrial nations to include some of the larger developing countries in the annual summit process 'since economic stability in the emerging market economies will increasingly affect the prosperity of the advanced economies as well'.[3] Sachs argues that, given India's economic power, democratic tradition and crucial role in global environmental issues, there is a strong case for the country's entry into the G-7 – ahead of the economically powerful but undemocratic China.[4]

Figure 2 *Purchasing-Power Parity (PPP) Comparisons*

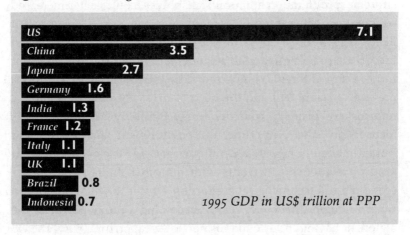

US	7.1
China	3.5
Japan	2.7
Germany	1.6
India	1.3
France	1.2
Italy	1.1
UK	1.1
Brazil	0.8
Indonesia	0.7

1995 GDP in US$ trillion at PPP

Source: World Trade Organisation, World Bank

The post-Cold War era offers a rare opportunity for India and the US to enhance strategic cooperation. This would have several benefits for both sides. It would ensure that India tempers its traditionally close relationship with Russia and that future Chinese military threats were balanced by a countervailing power. The US would benefit if it could rely on India to maintain stability in the region, to assist in countering terrorism and the narcotics trade, and to cooperate in peacekeeping operations. Deeper Indo-US co-operation would also strengthen the global non-proliferation regime.

India has not sold dual-use nuclear technology to potential proliferators, even when such deals would have been economically beneficial. Soon after India's 1974 nuclear test, Libya and Iraq asked for the explosive technology in return for 'attractive economic incentives'. Despite the fuel crisis in the 1970s, India refused.[5] Similarly, New Delhi withdrew its offer to sell a small (5MW) nuclear reactor to Iran when the US voiced proliferation concerns. In the sphere of chemical weapons, India was sensitive to the export of dual-use chemicals even before the CWC came into force. India has played a leading role in ensuring that Organisation for Prevention of Chemical Weapons (OPCW) conditions are established within the country and globally. India has become a reliable watch-dog, at least as far as chemical weapons are concerned.

Although Indian and US mutual interests, particularly in the strategic, proliferation and political spheres, could foster increased cooperation, this cannot be assured. Nor, for several reasons, is it likely to grow into a close strategic partnership overnight. India and the US are preoccupied with regional and domestic problems. For India, external threats compounded by internal security concerns, unstable government and the need to press ahead with economic reforms are primary considerations. Similarly, US attention is focused on inner-city crime, the environment and NATO- and Russia-related issues. As a result, neither side is clear about what kind of relationship it wants with the other. India wants closer economic and technological interaction – but is unwilling to forge a close strategic alliance for fear of becoming a proxy power in the region, or having to surrender its nuclear-weapon capability. The US too wants a closer relationship with India, but not at the cost of isolating Pakistan. Washington would be unwilling to part with state-of-the-art technology, even if it did not harbour proliferation concerns *vis-à-vis* India.

Thus, there are serious differences between the two countries, particularly over regional-proliferation issues. These are exaggerated by Cold War experiences and the presence of 'cold warriors' on both sides, who find it easier to fall back on their old confrontational and status-quo roles rather than embrace the post-Cold War possibilities. This makes smooth progress improbable.

On the other hand, the Indo-US relationship is unlikely to deteriorate to the point where it becomes based purely on a sanctions regime. For example, the US Commerce Department imposed export controls on four Indian establishments over India's missile and nuclear programme in July 1997.[6] Interestingly, the move was motivated more by the desire to warn errant US companies to follow US export guidelines than to punish India.[7] Moreover, India was not singled out: others such as Israel, China and Russia were also named.

This approach reflects the fact that an India-only sanctions regime would be counter-productive in strategic and non-proliferation terms. Despite the rudimentary nature of India's nuclear-weapon and missile capability, a sanctions regime is unlikely to dismantle its arsenal. While such a regime may succeed in slowing development of next-generation weapon and delivery systems, there is no guarantee that it would prevent it. Rather, sanctions would force India to become self-reliant in these areas and, therefore, out of reach of these regimes. Besides, an India-specific sanctions policy may remove any self-imposed restraints that New Delhi has shown in the export of sensitive nuclear and *commercial cooperation has momentum* missile technology. This would not only introduce another potential supplier into the clandestine market, but would also weaken existing non-proliferation arrangements.

While Indo-US relations are unlikely either to improve or deteriorate overnight, they are also unlikely to remain static. First, existing commercial cooperation has a momentum of its own, which is unlikely to be slowed in the foreseeable future. It may do so were India to reverse its economic-liberalisation policy, but this is unlikely, especially as the reform programme appears on track despite several changes of government. Commercial cooperation could also be at risk if the US imposed sanctions or made investment conditional on good proliferation behaviour. However, most US investment is not in sensitive areas and is, therefore, not under government purview. Market forces and expected returns are likely to dictate investment.

Second, even in sensitive areas, such as space applications and nuclear and military technology, currently substantial cooperation is expected to continue or deepen because it is mutually beneficial. Cooperation in these fields would strengthen the bonds between India and the West, provide the basis for a future strategic partnership, and create an economic and technical pool for large development projects beyond the capacity of any single country.

Third, India could provide not only cast-iron guarantees and unhindered access for verification of imported dual-use technology, but could also comply with MTCR guidelines. This has been proposed by several senior Indian scientists and is likely to be accepted officially.[8] According to one scientist, securing Indian agreement for more rigid control of its own exports would be in US interests, 'particularly since it would provide strong leverage for the US to use the same guidelines and approach for dealing with Pakistan and China'.[9] In addition, discussions on technology transfer and other issues through the JTG may eventually help to create a quid-pro-quo agreement between India and the US, particularly on non-proliferation. In the past, such discussions appear to have been conducted in academic isolation with little opportunity for follow-up. Now, however, while academic conferences provide the opportunities to advance radical ideas at a semi-official level, they can be officially handled and even elaborated through the DPG and JTG. Although it will be a slow process, it will be thorough.

Indo-US strategic cooperation can be deepened by building on existing mechanisms. A concerted effort towards a formal agreement is desirable, even though it would be arduous to achieve. Some of India's core interests will be maintained, but others may be compromised. A similar approach on the part of the US would be essential, not only to move the process of strategic cooperation forward, but also to achieve the goal of non-proliferation.

notes

Acknowledgements

The author would like to thank the Indian scientists, technologists, military personnel and bureaucrats who shared their experiences and enriched this study. He would also like to thank Stephen Cohen for his detailed comments, and the W. Alton Jones Foundation for its financial support.

Introduction

[1] The US accounted for 27% of the aggregate $5.14 billion Foreign Direct Investment (FDI) approvals in 1991–95. These figures are based on data from the Reserve Bank of India (RBI) and the Secretariat of Industry Approval (SIA), Ministry of Industry, Government of India. In 1994–95, the US took 19.1% of India's total exports and provided 10.1% of its imports. See http://www.indiaserver.com/embusa and http://www.meadev.gov.in/economy/intl.

[2] This view is held by, among others, DRDO head Dr A. P. J. Abdul Kalam. See Kalam, 'Combating the Technology Control Regime', *United Services Institute Journal*, vol. 126, no. 526, October–December 1996, pp. 438–46.

[3] 'Dealing successfully with the proliferation of weapons of mass destruction and missile delivery systems in South Asia will require that the US and others take into account both Indian and Pakistani domestic political concerns and regional security threat perceptions, including those extending beyond the two countries themselves.' *Report to Congress: Update on Progress Towards Regional Nonproliferation in South Asia* (Washington DC: US Government Printing Office, 1997), p. 8.

[4] 'India Integrating Fast into World Economy: WB [World Bank]', *The Statesman*, 8 May 1996.

[5] Remarks by then US Commerce Secretary Ronald H. Brown at the Big Emerging Markets Conference, Opening Session, Washington DC, 24 July 1995. See http://www.stat-usa.gov/bems/remarks.html.

Although the RBI reported a slow-down in industrial and export growth rates in 1996–97, GDP growth is likely to remain at 6.8% a year. See 'Reserve Bank of India Projects GDP at 6.8%', *BBC Summary of World Broadcasts (SWB)/ Far East* 0473 WA/1, 12 February 1997.
[6] Washington acknowledges that US firms face growing international competition in all sectors of the Indian market. Germany, Japan and the UK 'furnish roughly 30% of India's imports although no one country exceeds 8.4%'. See 'Big Emerging Markets: India', http:// www.stat-usa.gov/bems/bemsind/ bemsind.html. Italy's Fiat car-maker in July 1997 announced a five-year, $1bn investment. See 'Fiat Earmarks $1bn for Ventures in India', *Indian Express*, 21 July 1997.
[7] According to one estimate, US technology accounts for 23% of the total imported by India. See Stephen Mintz, 'The Case for India as a Technology Partner', brochure for consultancy company Global Exchange of Technology Inc., Burke, VA, 1997, p. 2.
[8] The term 'strategic' normally relates only to a military partnership. The 'grand strategy' components could include an economic partnership, technology transfer and a shared global outlook on politics (particularly the nature of government), the environment, human rights and even nuclear non-proliferation.
[9] This cooperation could be less than an alliance, but more than a series of spells of cooperation. It could be strategic in some areas, but not in others; it could be an economic and ideological relationship without a military

component. Closer ties in these areas may create mutual dependencies that would spill over into alliances and military policy.
[10] Incentives the US could offer are the subject of a forthcoming IISS study by Virginia Foran.

Chapter 1

[1] This has prompted scholars such as Scott Sagan to endorse the 'multicausality' approach to proliferation-behaviour studies. See Sagan, 'Why Do States Build Nuclear Weapons? Three Models in Search of a Bomb', *International Security*, vol. 18, no. 3, Winter 1996–97, pp. 54–86.
[2] These include Ashok Kapur, *India's Nuclear Option: Atomic Diplomacy and Decision Making* (New York: Praeger Publishers, 1976); T. T. Poulouse (ed.), *Perspectives of India's Nuclear Policy* (New Delhi: Lancer Publishers, 1978); Shyam Bhatia, *India's Nuclear Bomb* (Ghaziabad: Vikas Publications, 1979); Rodney W. Jones, 'India', in Jozef Goldblat (ed.), *Non-Proliferation: The Why and the Wherefore* (London: Taylor & Francis, 1985), pp. 101–16; Itty Abraham, 'India's Strategic Enclave: Civilian Scientists and Military Technologies', *Armed Forces and Society*, vol. 18, no. 2, Winter 1992, pp. 231–52; Mitchell Reiss, *Bridled Ambition: Why Countries Constrain Their Nuclear Capabilities* (Washington DC: Woodrow Wilson International Center for Scholars, 1995). See also George Perkovich, *India's Ambiguous Bomb*, PhD dissertation, University of Virginia, May 1997; Lavoy, *Learning to Live with the Bomb: India and Nuclear Weapons*

1947–1974, PhD dissertation, University of California, Berkeley, 1997; Waheguru Pal Singh Sidhu, *The Development of an Indian Nuclear Doctrine Since 1980*, PhD dissertation, University of Cambridge, February 1997.

[3] Dennis Kux, *India and the United States: Estranged Democracies* (Washington DC: National Defense University, 1992), pp. 207–8.

[4] Raju G. C. Thomas, *South Asian Security in the 1990s*, Adelphi Paper 278 (London: Brassey's for the IISS, 1993), p. 3.

[5] Indian Ministry of Defence, *Ministry of Defence Annual Report 1996–97* (New Delhi: Government of India, 1997), p. 2.

[6] For a contemporary account of the military's concerns over China's nuclear weapons, see Major General D. Som Dutt, *The Defence of India's Northern Border*, Adelphi Paper 25 (London: Institute for Strategic Studies, 1966), and *India and the Bomb*, Adelphi Paper 30 (London: Institute for Strategic Studies, 1966).

[7] By 1965, India was producing fissile material from the 40MW CIRUS reactor and was also able to reprocess plutonium from it.

[8] See Brigadier D. Banerjee, 'China's Emerging Nuclear Doctrine: A Prognostication', *Combat*, vol. 16, no. 1, April 1989, pp. 3–14; Air Commodore Jasjit Singh, 'The Strategic Deterrent Option', *Strategic Analysis*, vol. 12, no. 9, September 1989, p. 587; Colonels A. Sahgal and T. Singh, 'Nuclear Threat from China: An Appraisal', *Trishul*, vol. 6, no. 2, January 1994, pp. 27–38.

[9] IISS, *The Military Balance 1988–1989* (London: Brassey's for the IISS, 1989), p. 149.

[10] Sahgal and Singh, 'Nuclear Threat from China', pp. 32, 36. See also Robert S. Norris, Andrew S. Burrows and Richard W. Fieldhouse, *Nuclear Weapons Databook Volume V: British, French, and Chinese Nuclear Weapons* (Boulder, CO: Westview Press, 1994), pp. 338–41 and Figure 6.10, pp. 346–47.

[11] R. Chandran, 'New Chinese Missiles Target India: US Daily', *Times of India*, 11 July 1997.

[12] Simon Henderson, 'Pakistan's Atomic Bomb', *Foreign Report*, 12 January 1989, quoted in David Albright and Mark Hibbs, 'Pakistan's Bomb: Out of the Closet', *Bulletin of the Atomic Scientists*, vol. 48, no. 4, July–August 1992, pp. 38–43.

[13] See Bill Gertz, 'Pakistan–China Deal for Missiles Exposed', *Washington Times*, 7 September 1994; R. Jeffrey Smith and Thomas W. Lippman, 'Pakistan M-11 Funding Is Reported', *Washington Post*, 8 September 1994, p. A32; Michael Klare, *Rogue States and Nuclear Outlaws* (New York: Hill and Wang, 1995), pp. 152, 191.

[14] James Woolsey's testimony before the Senate Governmental Affairs Committee, 24 February 1993.

[15] R. Jeffrey Smith and David B. Ottaway, 'Spy Photos Suggest China Missile Trade', *Washington Post*, 3 July 1995, p. A1; Smith, 'China Linked to Pakistani Missile Plant', *Washington Post*, 23 August 1996, pp. A1, A23, cited in 'India–Pakistan Nuclear and Missile Proliferation: Background, Status and Issues for US Policy', *Congressional Research Service Report for Congress* (Washington DC: US Government Printing Office, 1996), pp. 20–21. See also Douglas Waller,

'The Secret Missile Deal', *Time*, 30 June 1997, p. 58.

[16] This has been reiterated in Indian Ministry of Defence, *Ministry of Defence Annual Report 1996–97*, p. 2.

[17] Klare, *Rogue States*, pp. 152, 191.

[18] Shekhar Gupta, 'Nuclear Weapons in the Subcontinent', in *Defence and Insecurity in Southern Asia: The Conventional and Nuclear Dimensions*, Occasional Paper 21 (Washington DC: Henry L. Stimson Center, 1995), pp. 45–46.

[19] Interview with General Beg by Michael Krepon, Rawalpindi, May 1994.

[20] See R. Jeffrey Smith, 'Pakistan Warns India on Missiles', *Washington Post*, 4 June 1997, p. A20; K. K. Katyal, 'Prithvi Missile Merely Stored at Jalandhar', *The Hindu*, 8 June 1997.

[21] Benazir Bhutto's statement reported in *The Muslim*, 6 February 1989.

[22] The reconstruction of the 1971 *USS Enterprise* episode is based on several sources, including Henry Kissinger, *The White House Years* (London: Weidenfield and Nicolson, 1979), pp. 905, 911–12; Admiral S. N. Kohli, 'The Geopolitical and Strategic Considerations that Necessitate the Expansion and Modernisation of the Indian Navy', *Indian Defence Review*, January 1989, p. 38; Vice-Admiral Mihir K. Roy, *War in the Indian Ocean* (New Delhi: Lancer Publishers, 1995), pp. 212–13; Captain Ranjit Rai, 'Foreign Interference in the Indian Ocean 1971 Repeat Performance – A Research', *United Services Institute Journal*, vol. 112, no. 420, October–December 1982, pp. 316–20. See also Stephen P. Cohen, *Perceptions, Influence and Weapons Proliferation in South Asia*, report prepared for the US Department of State Bureau of Intelligence and Research, Contract No. 1722–920184, Washington DC, August 1979, p. 4.

[23] The phrase 'raising the cost of intervention' was coined by K. Subrahmanyan in *Our National Security*, Monograph No. 3 (London: Economic and Scientific Research Foundation, 1972), p. xxi.

[24] Klare, *Rogue States*, p. 208.

[25] In practice, the AEC chairman has the power to formulate, initiate and implement India's nuclear programme in total secrecy and is responsible only to the Prime Minister, who is also the Cabinet Minister responsible for atomic energy. See Dhirendra Sharma, *India's Nuclear Estate* (New Delhi: Lancer Publishers, 1983), p. 149.

[26] *IAEA Press Release PR 97/6*, Vienna, 24 April 1997.

[27] See Stephen P. Cohen and Richard L. Park, *India: Emergent Power?* (New York: Crane, Russak & Co., 1978), pp. xxi, 91; Cohen, *Perceptions, Influence and Weapons Proliferation in South Asia*, p. 58.

[28] Shekhar Gupta, *India Redefines its Role*, Adelphi Paper 293 (Oxford: Oxford University Press for the IISS, 1995), p. 46.

[29] R. Chidambaram, A. Kakodkar and P. Rodrigues, 'Nuclear Technology: Power to the People', *IEEE Spectrum*, vol. 31, no. 3, p. 36.

[30] According to one assessment, the 'failure of the Indian civilian nuclear power industry' has forced it to 'form an alliance with the pro-bomb lobby to justify its existence and funding after its failure to avoid cost overruns and prevent safety problems in domestic energy programs'. See Scott Sagan, 'The Causes of Nuclear Proliferation', *Current History*, vol. 96, no. 109, April 1997, p. 154.

[31] Waheguru Pal Singh Sidhu, 'India's Nuclear Tests: Technical and Military Imperatives', *Jane's Intelligence Review*, vol. 8, no. 4, April 1996, pp. 170–73.

[32] Rahul Roy-Chaudhary, 'Defence Research and Development in India', in *Asian Strategic Review* (New Delhi: Institute for Defence Studies and Analysis, 1995), p. 226.

[33] India's space programme was only formally organised in 1962 with the establishment of the Indian National Committee for Space Research (INCOSPAR) under the DAE. INCOSPAR became the ISRO in 1969.

[34] See Timothy McCarthy, 'India: The Emerging Missile Power', *Defence Journal*, vol. 19, nos 9–10, September–October 1993, p. 61.

[35] *Indian Space Program*, Cable to US Department of Defense No. 30510, US Embassy Political Section, New Delhi, 6 January 1988, paragraph 62, cited in Timothy McCarthy, 'India: The Emerging Missile Power', in William C. Potter and Harlan W. Jencks (eds), *The International Missile Bazaar: The New Suppliers' Network* (Boulder, CO: Westview Press, 1994), p. 205.

[36] A declassified US State Department Telegram from the US Embassy in New Delhi in December 1987 noted in paragraph 96: 'And though the organisations are competitive, it is most natural for scientists and engineers working on similar problems (particularly if working for the same employer-of-last-resort) to discuss problems and success, sharing information about their projects.' Telegram No. 31294, National Security Archives, Washington DC.

[37] One of the most comprehensive semi-official accounts of the missile programme can be found in Indranil Banerjie, 'The Integrated Guided Missile Development Programme', *Indian Defence Review*, July 1990, pp. 99–109. For a discussion of the two strategic missiles, see Major-General V. J. Sundaram, 'Surface-to-Surface Missiles Come of Age in India', *Artillery Journal*, 1990, pp. 53–55; R. N. Agarwal, 'Agni', in *ibid.*, pp. 56–57. See also Stephen M. Flank, 'Reconstructing Rockets: The Politics of Developing Military Technology in Brazil, India and Israel', PhD dissertation, Massachusetts Institute of Technology, 1993.

[38] 'Tactical' refers to the immediate battlefield and to weapons used against military formations to determine the outcome of a battle; 'strategic' refers to weapons that could be used against the war-making capacity of a nation, such as command centres, storage depots, economic and population targets and troop concentrations and staging areas behind the battlefield. However, given Pakistan's size, this distinction blurs. 'Nuclear-capable' is used to denote a delivery system with the payload, throw-weight and physical dimensions theoretically to be armed with a nuclear weapon. Technically, a missile with a diameter of one metre and a payload of one ton can be configured to carry a first- or second-generation nuclear weapon, which is about one ton in weight and one metre in diameter.

[39] Author's interview with Dr Kalam, Hyderabad, October 1990.

[40] Author's interview with Dr Arunachalam, Pittsburgh, PA, February 1997.

[41] India encountered a similar

situation in 1978, when the US
passed the Nuclear Non-
Proliferation Act (NNPA) and
abrogated a bilateral nuclear
cooperation agreement in response
to India's 1974 nuclear test. The US
move was an attempt to ensure
that non-weapon states would
accept NPT-type safeguards,
whether or not they were parties to
the Treaty. See Davis, 'Non-
proliferation Regimes: Policies to
Control the Spread of Nuclear,
Chemical and Biological Weapons
and Missiles', *Congressional Research
Service Report for Congress*
(Washington DC: US Government
Printing Office, 1993), p. 20.
[42] Author's interview with Dr
Kalam, October 1990.
[43] Raj Chengappa, 'The Missile
Man', *India Today*, 15 April 1994,
p. 44.
[44] Notable projects which have
slipped include the *Arjun* main
battle tank (MBT) and the light
combat aircraft (LCA). The MBT
project was commissioned in 1974;
the first prototype was planned for
1980. The design was finalised only
in July 1996, and the MBT is
scheduled to enter service in 2002.
The LCA was commissioned in
1983 and was to replace the MiG-21
fleet by the mid-1990s. However,
the first flight is slated for late 1997
and the aircraft is now scheduled
to enter service in 2005–7.
[45] Author's interview with Dr
Kalam, October 1990.
[46] Indian Ministry of Defence,
*Ministry of Defence Annual Report
1996–97*, p. 55.
[47] See R. Chidambaram and V.
Ashok, 'Embargo Regimes and
Impact', in Deepa Ollapally and S.
Rajagopal (eds), *Nuclear
Cooperation: Challenges and Prospects*
(Bangalore: National Institute of

Advanced Studies, 1997), p. 74.
[48] *Ibid*.
[49] 'Appendix B: Complete Results
and Tabular Data of the Kroc
Institute Opinion Survey', in David
Cortright and Amitabh Mattoo
(eds), *India and the Bomb: Public
Opinion and Nuclear Options* (Notre
Dame, IN: University of Notre
Dame Press, 1996), p. 118.
[50] Cited in Thomas W. Graham,
India's Nuclear Program: A Briefing,
unpublished background paper for
The Asia Society, New York, 1994.
[51] Cortright and Mattoo (eds), *India
and the Bomb*, p. 11.
[52] Dutt, *The Defence of India's
Northern Border* and *India and the
Bomb*; Lieutenant-General
Krishnaswami Sundarji (ed.),
*Effects of Nuclear Asymmetry on
Conventional Deterrence*, Combat
Papers No. 1, and Sudarji (ed.),
*Nuclear Weapons in Third World
Context*, Combat Papers No. 2
(Mhow, India: College of Combat,
1981); Stephen Peter Rosen,
*Societies and Military Power: India
and Its Armies*, (Ithaca, NY: Cornell
University Press, 1996), p. 251.
Rosen argues that 'the civilian
leadership has fought a long and
difficult struggle with the Indian
military to decide who would
control nuclear weapons and how
they would be used. This struggle
was resolved in favour of the
civilians.'
[53] Sidhu, 'India's Nuclear Tests',
pp. 170–73.
[54] Manoj Joshi, 'Operation
Defreeze', *India Today*, 11 August
1997, p. 68; Lieutenant-General J. F.
R. Jacob publicly called for a
missile with a range of at least
5,000km.
[55] Gupta, *India Redefines its Role*,
p. 46.
[56] See Kapur, *India's Nuclear Option*,

p. 198, and Bhatia, *India's Nuclear Bomb*, pp. 153–54. This view is endorsed by Sagan. See 'The Causes of Nuclear Proliferation', pp. 153–54.
57 US officials shared this assessment. See 'Nuclear Proliferation in South Asia: Containing the Threat', *Staff Report to the United States Senate Committee on Foreign Relations* (Washington DC: US Government Printing Office, 1988), p. 2.
58 *Times of India*, 22 July 1989.
59 *BJP Manifesto 1996*, New Delhi, April 1996.
60 Ashok Kapur, 'The CTBT Experience', *The Hindu*, 24 September 1996.
61 Kanti Bajpai, 'India in a Diplomatic Soup', *Outlook*, 4 September 1996, p. 45.
62 Kapur, 'The CTBT Experience'. Kapur argues that Rao's private deal with the US was similar to the backdoor pressure applied on Indira Gandhi in 1967–68 over the NPT debate. Gandhi, who initially favoured the NPT, later rejected it, possibly because of the strength of domestic public opinion against the Treaty.
63 R. Jeffrey Johnson, 'The In-Comprehensive Test Ban', *Bulletin of the Atomic Scientists*, vol. 52, no. 6, November–December 1996, p. 32. One report suggests that a device was placed in a shaft at Pokhran. See Manoj Joshi, 'In the Shadow of Fear', *India Today*, 21 July 1997, p. 62.
64 See, for example: 'NYT report on N-Test A Big Lie: Ramanna', *Times of India*, 17 December 1995; 'Opposition Calls for Rebuff to US Pressure', *Indian Express*, 17 December 1995; C. Raja Mohan, 'India's Nuclear Option', *The Hindu*, 20 December 1995; Praful Bidwai, 'India Disarmament: New Turn to Indian Test Ban Debate', *Inter Press Service*, 28 December 1995; Raj Chengappa, 'Testing Times', *India Today*, December 1995, pp. 46–51; Sunil Narula, 'Pressure Tactics', *Outlook*, 3 January 1996, pp. 30–31; Kanti Bajpai, 'India Should Give Up the Nuclear Option', *Times of India*, 24 January 1996; 'India's Nuclear Options', *Frontline*, 26 January 1996, pp. 4–21; Bajpai, 'Thinking the Unthinkable', *Security Technology and Arms Control News*, February 1996; A. M. Gupta, 'Nuclear Choice: Facing up to New Pressure', *The Statesman Weekly*, 30 March 1996.
65 Chengappa, 'Testing Times', pp. 46–51.
66 S. Viswam, 'India's Reservations on CTBT', *India Perspectives*, September 1996, p. 24.
67 *Ibid.*, p. 25.
68 See *Preventing Nuclear Proliferation in South Asia* (New York: The Asia Society, 1995), p. 34.
69 Air Commodore Jasjit Singh, 'Implications of Ballistic Missile Defences: An Indian Perspective', paper presented to the conference 'The Implications of Ballistic Missile Defences for Crisis Stability and Regional Security', Wilton Park, Sussex, 29 April–3 May 1996, p. 7.
70 *Ibid.*
71 V. S. Arunachalam, L. V. Krishnan and R. Tongia, 'Nuclear Power in India – The Road Ahead', unpublished paper, Department of Engineering and Public Policy, Carnegie Mellon University, Pittsburgh, PA, 1997, p. 8.
72 S. Saraf, 'An Agonising Wait', *Financial Times*, 19 June 1997.
73 Emma Duncan, 'They Can't Let Go', *The Economist*, 21 January 1995, p. 20. For a detailed study of

the Dabhol case, see Rajesh Kumar, 'The Development of Strategic Alliances in a Chaotic Environment: Lessons from the Power Sector in India', unpublished paper, Eindhoven Institute of Technology, 1996.
[74] Inder Kumar Gujral, 'Friendship With The World? Yes, But Not At The Cost Of India', *Inter Press Service*, 2 June 1997, http://www.meadev.gov.in/news/clippings/19970602/aa.htm. The Gujral doctrine was also aimed at consolidating old ties with Moscow and building new business-driven relations with Washington. See 'South Block Sees the World in Concentric Circles', *Reuters*, 19 March 1997, http://www.meadev.gov.in/news/clippings/19970320/aa1.htm.
[75] 'Security Council Games', *Indian Express*, 21 July 1997.
[76] Congressmen who have pressed India's case include Benjamin Gilman, head of the influential International Relations Committee of the House of Representatives. See 'US Congressman Advocates Seat for India in UN Council', *The Hindu*, 16 August 1997.
[77] Author's interview with former AEC Chairman Dr Iyengar, Mumbai, India, 1997.
[78] Saritha Rai, 'Farewell to Arms', *India Today*, 30 April 1997, pp. 56–57.

Chapter 2

[1] For details of Indo-US cooperation in this period, see Satu P. Limaye, *US–Indian Relations: The Pursuit of Accommodation* (Boulder, CO: Westview Press, 1993); M. S. Swaminathan (ed.), *Wheat Revolution: A Dialogue* (Madras: Macmillan (India) Ltd, 1993); K. Santhanam, 'Indian Defence Technology Infrastructure and Prospects of Indo-US Cooperation', paper presented at the 'Indo-US Defense Workshop', National Defense University, Washington DC, 19–21 September 1989; K. Santhanam and Jasjit Singh, 'Confidence Restoring Measures for Indo-US Commerce in Controlled Commodities', in Francine R. Frankel (ed.), *Bridging the Non-Proliferation Divide: The United States and India* (Lanham, MD: University Press of America, 1995), pp. 319–33, and V. S. Arunachalam, 'India and the United States: Issues in Science and Technology', paper presented at the Meeting on Technology Transfer and Weapons Proliferation at the National Institute of Advanced Studies, Bangalore, 17–19 January 1994, p. 7. See also Brahma Chellaney, *Nuclear Proliferation: The US–India Conflict* (New Delhi: Orient Longman, 1993).
[2] Apart from the US contribution to India's 'green revolution' and the supply of fuel to the Tarapur nuclear reactor, India and the US also cooperated in space research with experiments in sounding rockets launched from the Thumba Equatorial Rocket Launching Station (TERLS) in India.
[3] The US decision to embargo arms to India and Pakistan during the 1965 war was another factor behind New Delhi's self-reliance drive.
[4] Report by Dr Jerome Weisner to John Palfrey, Declassified State Department Telegram No. 2054, 21 January 1965, Lyndon B. Johnson Library, Austin, TX. Weisner suggests 'various technical things

that could be done. I have discussed the possibility of a small satellite, plowshare experiments, tropical weather studies, Asian-region ground water development, collaborative research on thorium fuel and fast reactors and further cooperative activities on technical education'.

5 Michael Edwardes, 'India, Pakistan and Nuclear Weapons', *International Affairs*, vol. 43, no. 4, October 1967, p. 658.
6 Ambassador John G. Dean, 'Indo-US Relations: Fulfilling the Promise', cited in Limaye, *US–Indian Relations*, p. 165.
7 Arunachalam, 'India and the United States', p. 21.
8 The STI was to become the model for technology cooperation with other countries. In 1986, President Reagan and his Brazilian counterpart, José Sarney, signed a similar initiative. It is likely that the Indo-US MOU was derived from the US–Israeli model.
9 Limaye, *US–Indian Relations*, pp. 27–30, 40–1.
10 'When informed Mrs Gandhi retorted, "What kind of people are these Soviets who said that they have no such thing as a MiG-29 in October [1983] and agree to their manufacture in India by December of the same year?"' Ramaswamy Venkataraman, *My Presidential Years* (New Delhi: HarperCollins Publishers India, 1994), pp. 81–82.
11 Santosh Mehrota, *India and the Soviet Union: Trade and Technology Transfer* (Cambridge: Cambridge University Press, 1990), p. 21.
12 *Ibid.*, p. 23.
13 Kux, *Estranged Democracies*, p. 381. Ironically, this period also saw the single largest Indian procurement of Soviet military hardware, including MiG-29, IL-76 and An-32 aircraft, Mi-35 helicopter gunships, BMP-I and II infantry combat vehicles, T-72 MBTs and the EK-877M *Kilo* and *Charlie*-I submarines.
14 Author's interview with Dr Arunachalam, February 1997. Ustinov apparently offered to build the aircraft on India's behalf, but the DRDO was adamant that it wanted to undertake the programme itself. The DRDO's stance was supported by Prime Minister Indira Gandhi.
15 See Stephen P. Cohen, 'The Reagan Administration and India', in Harold A. Gould and Sumit Ganguly (eds), *The Hope and the Reality: US–Indian Relations from Roosevelt to Reagan* (Boulder, CO: Westview Press, 1992), p. 141. For details of the US coalitions that made the Reagan administration's overtures to India possible, see also Limaye, *The Pursuit of Accommodation*, pp. 32–48.
16 Cohen, 'The Reagan Administration and India', p. 143.
17 Kux, *Estranged Democracies*, p. 402.
18 Author's interview with Dr Arunachalam, February 1997.
19 According to one estimate, from 1980–81 onwards, the DRDO's expenditure equalled and then surpassed that of the DAE and DOS. In addition, the DRDO's share of total defence expenditure increased from 2.6% in 1983 to 5% in 1989. See Santhanam, 'Indian Defence Technology Infrastructure', pp. 2, 6.
20 V. S. Arunachalam, 'The Acquisitions Game: An Analysis of the Demand Side of the Game', *Harvard International Review*, vol. 17, no. 1, Winter 1994–95, p. 73.
21 Santhanam and Singh, 'Confidence Restoring Measures',

p. 332.

22 Indo-US high-technology cooperation has much in common with Israeli–US cooperation in this sphere. See, for example, Dov S. Zakheim, *Flight of the Lavi: Inside a US–Israeli Crisis* (McLean, VA: Brassey's (US) Inc., 1996).

23 Author's interview with Global Exchange Technology President Stephen Mintz, Washington DC, February 1997.

24 Limaye, *The Pursuit of Accommodation*, pp. 170–71.

25 Santhanam and Singh, 'Confidence Restoring Measures', pp. 324–25.

26 *Ibid.*, p. 325. Although the MTCR came into effect three years after the MOU, it appears to have been 'cooperatively addressed in a bilateral mode', as it did not adversely affect the MOU.

27 Limaye, *The Pursuit of Accommodation*, p. 202.

28 *Import Certificate Procedures Under the Indo-US MOU on Technology Transfer* (New Delhi: Ministry of External Affairs, 1985), p. 2.

29 Santhanam, 'Indian Defence Technology Infrastructure', p. 15.

30 Arunachalam, 'India and the United States', p. 22.

31 Author's interview with Professor Stephen P. Cohen, former State Department official under President Reagan, Urbana, IL, February 1997.

32 See 'India to Buy US Aircraft Engine', *Far Eastern Economic Review*, 9 October 1986, p. 12, and 'High Technology Arms Sales Arouse Concerns', *Washington Post*, 6 December 1986, p. A20.

33 Author's interview with Dr R. Krishnan, Bangalore, April 1997.

34 Stuart Auerbach, 'US To Let India Buy Supercomputer', *Washington Post*, 1 November 1986, p. C1.

35 David E. Sanger, 'US Lets India Buy Computer', *New York Times*, 27 March 1987, p. 1.

36 Kux, *Estranged Democracies*, pp. 410–11.

37 White House Statement on 'New Initiatives in Indo-US Relations', 20 October 1987.

38 Author's interview with DRDO Chief Adviser (Technologies) Santhanam, April 1997, New Delhi. See also Santhanam and Singh, 'Confidence Restoring Measures', p. 326.

39 Santhanam, 'Indian Defence Technology Infrastructure', p. 15.

40 R. J. Augustus, 'Technology Transfer to Indian Defence Research and Development Laboratories Through Indo-US Defence Cooperation: Issues and Opportunities', PhD dissertation, Pacific Western University, 1996.

41 *The Hindu*, 23 October 1987.

42 Author's interview with Indian space scientists, Bangalore, April 1997, and with Van H. Van Diepen, Director, Office of Chemical, Biological and Missile Nonproliferation, Bureau of Political–Military Affairs, Washington DC, February 1997.

43 David B. Ottaway, 'Bush Administration Debates Sale of Missile-testing Device to India', *Washington Post*, 28 May 1989, p. A8.

44 Kalam, 'Combating the Technology Control Regime', p. 441.

45 Augustus, 'Technology Transfer', p. 190.

46 Author's interview with senior Pentagon official, February 1997, Washington DC.

47 Memorandum of Conversation, Department of State, 22 February 1965, Lyndon B. Johnson Library, Austin, TX.

[48] *Ibid.*

[49] Department of State Telegram No. 04656, 12 January 1965, Lyndon B. Johnson Library, Austin, TX. Scientific projects for which the US was willing to offer assistance included plutonium and thorium recycling, and developing the Trombay regional centre for studying and training in peaceful uses of nuclear energy.

[50] *Ibid.*

[51] Message from Dr Weisner to US Secretary of State, Telegram No. 15567, 21 January 1965, Lyndon B. Johnson Library, Austin, TX.

[52] *Aide-mémoire* presented to the AEC, Bombay, 16 November 1970, National Security Archives, Washington DC.

[53] M. Z. I. Cheema, *Indian Nuclear Strategy: 1947–1991*, PhD dissertation, University of London, 1991, p. 216. This assurance, however, depended on the success of US efforts to prevent Pakistan from acquiring a nuclear-weapon capability. See also Virginia Foran and Leonard Spector, 'Application of Incentives to Nuclear Proliferation', in David Cortright (ed.), *The Price of Peace: Incentives and International Conflict Prevention* (forthcoming), p. 40. The authors claim that there was an explicit agreement between the US and Pakistan under which General Zia ul-Haq pledged to curtail Pakistan's bid for nuclear arms in return for US economic and military assistance.

[54] Sidhu, *The Development of an Indian Nuclear Doctrine Since 1980*, pp. 204–5.

[55] Santhanam and Singh, 'Confidence Restoring Measures', p. 332.

[56] Jyoti Malhotra, 'Relations after Raphel', *Indian Express*, 18 July 1997. See also Malhotra, 'US May Give India Leeway [on] NPT', *Indian Express*, 24 June 1997.

Chapter 3

[1] *A New US Policy Towards India and Pakistan*, report of the Independent Task Force sponsored by the Council on Foreign Relations (CFR), Washington DC, 1997, p. 25.

[2] Author's interviews with Dr Richard Haass, Director of Foreign Policy Studies at the Brookings Institution and Chairman of the CFR Independent Task Force, and with a senior Pentagon official, Washington DC, February 1997.

[3] C. Rammanohar Reddy, 'WTO Likely to be Globalised by Next Year', *The Hindu*, 3 July 1997.

[4] Thomas, 'South Asian Security in the 1990s', p. 9.

[5] QRs are allowed under Article 18B of the WTO, which permits developing countries to restrict imports for balance-of-payments reasons. See Rammanohar Reddy, 'Few Takers for Indian offer at WTO', *The Hindu*, 1 July 1997; 'Govt Urged to Counter WTO Challenge', *The Hindu*, 23 July 1997; 'Special 301: India Regrets US Decision', *The Hindu*, 1 May 1997.

[6] See Kumar, 'The Development of Strategic Alliances in a Chaotic Environment'.

[7] The size of the Indian middle-class market has been estimated at 250–300 million and around 100m. See Emma Duncan, 'Hello World – Economic Reform Has Helped, But India's Government Is Still Frustrating Its People's Ambitions', *The Economist*, 21 January 1995; Charubala Annuncio, 'The Discovery of India', *Outlook*, 23 July 1997, p. 54.

8 Prem Shankar Jha, 'India's Failing Economy – II', *The Hindu*, 9 July 1997.

9 Augustus, 'Technology Transfer', p. 193.

10 'India, US to Work in Hi-tech Areas', *The Hindu*, 25 October 1996.

11 This assessment is drawn from the experiences of senior technocrats closely involved with the formulation and implementation of the MOU. See Santhanam and Singh, 'Confidence Restoring Measures', pp. 329–30.

12 A. A. Pikayev, L. S. Spector, E. V. Kirichenko and R. Gibson, 'The Soviet–Russian Sale of Cryogenic Rocket Technology to India and Russia's Adherence to the Missile Technology Control Regime', unpublished paper.

13 'US Approval of Chinese Launches Determined by Value of Satellites', *Aviation Week and Space Technology*, 3 October 1988, p. 25.

14 One exception is high-resolution satellite imagery which, although primarily used for resource management and town planning, also has military applications.

15 See 'US Approval of Chinese Launches', p. 25.

16 See Andrea Ahles, 'Foreign Trade Agreements Threaten US Launch Industry', *Defense Daily*, 14 June 1996; Randy Ridley, 'The Battle for the Launch Pad: Satellite Launching Companies Compete Internationally', *Satellite Communications*, June 1994, p. 33.

17 See Hormuz P. Mama, 'India's IRS Family Comes of Age', *Interavia*, vol. 51, no. 602, 1 August 1996, p. 64.

18 S. Krishnaprasad, 'IRS Data will Earn $10 Million in Forex', *Indian Express*, 9 April 1997, p. 4.

19 I am grateful to John C. Baker for this valuable collection of facts and assessment.

20 Author's interview with N. Sampath, Executive Director of Antarix Corporation Limited, Bangalore, April 1997.

21 Sanctions were imposed on 11 May 1992 under the US Arms Export Control Act and the Export Administration Act.

22 Private communication with a former member of the US National Security Council, June 1997, who conveyed to senior Indian diplomats at a luncheon in Washington DC that the US was willing to offer incentives if India gave up its quest for cryogenic engines. The Indian diplomats rejected the offer outright.

23 This test was conducted on 19 February 1994. India also test-launched its PSLV in September 1993.

24 Author's interview with N. Sampath, April 1997.

25 Author's interview with Lisa Shaffer, Washington DC, April 1997.

26 Warren Ferster, 'India, United States Near Data Agreement', *Space News*, 1–7 April 1996.

27 *Ibid*.

28 'N-power will get High Priority', *Times of India*, 23 January 1997.

29 S. S. Banyal, 'Nuclear Power Plans: Panel Flays Govt's "Ad Hoc" Approach', *The Hindustan Times*, 12 March 1997.

30 Arunachalam, Krishnan and Tongia, 'Nuclear Power in India – The Road Ahead'.

31 Nirmola George, 'India Wooing Foreign Nuclear Companies to Set Up Shop', *Indian Express*, 20 June 1997.

32 Atul Aneja, 'India, Pak Can Share Power: US Report', *The Hindu*, 19 June 1997.

33 Author's interview with Richard

Haass, February 1997.

Conclusion

[1] Air Commodore Jasjit Singh, 'Prospects for Nuclear Proliferation', in Serge Sur (ed.), *Nuclear Deterrence: Problems and Perspectives in the 1990s* (New York: United Nations Institute for Disarmament Research, 1993), p. 66.
[2] James Walsh, 'One World Divided', *Time*, 7 July 1997, p. 42.
[3] Jeffrey Sachs, 'New Members Please Apply', *ibid.*, p. 45.
[4] *Ibid.*
[5] See V. S. Arunachalam, 'Defence, Technology and Development – The Indian Experience', in Desmond Ball and Helen Wilson (eds), *New Technology: Implications for Regional and Australian Security*, Canberra Papers on Strategy and Defence, no. 76 (Canberra: Australian National University, 1991), p. 90. The CIA's Director of Central Intelligence's June 1997 biannual report does not list India as a supplier, even though it sought to acquire some items for its missile programme. See *The Acquisition of Technology Relating to Weapons of Mass Destruction and Advanced Conventions/Munitions, July–December 1996*, http://www.fas.org/irp/cia/wmd.htm.
[6] The four establishments were: Bharat Electronics; BARC; Bharat Rare Earths; and the Indira Gandhi Center for Atomic Research. See 'Washington is the Problem – US Export Controls More a Setback', *Indian Express*, 4 July 1997.
[7] Chidanand Rajghatta, 'US Firm Prosecuted for Hi-tech Exports to India', *Indian Express*, 20 July 1997.
[8] V. S. Arunachalam, 'Of Machines and Men: Technology and Social Responsibility in the Age of Weapons of Mass Destruction', paper presented at the Aspen Institute Seminar 'The Proliferation Threat of Weapons of Mass Destruction and US Security Interests', Aspen, CO, August 1996, p. 7. See also Brahma Chellaney 'An Indian Critique of US Exports Control', *Orbis*, vol. 38, no. 3, Summer 1994, p. 452.
[9] Augustus, 'Technology Transfer', p. 196.